THE AMERICAN
ARCHITECTURAL
PHOTOGRAPHER

Profiles of the Top Talent in Architectural Photography

RWP
RP

Elite Editions Library

First published in the United States of America by:
Rockport Publishers, Inc.
146 Granite Street
Rockport, Massachusetts 01966
Telephone: 508.546.9590
Fax: 508.546.7141
Telex: 5106019284 ROCKORT PUB

Resource World Publications, Inc.
209 West Central Street
Suite 204
Natick, MA 01760
Telephone: 508.651.7000
Fax: 508.651.9950

Other Distribution by:
Rockport Publishers, Inc.
Rockport, Massachusetts 01966

ISBN 1-56496-073-0

10 9 8 7 6 5 4 3 2 1

Project Director: Arthur Furst
Editorial/Project Coordinator: Jonathan T. Frederick
Design/Layout: Laura Herrmann
Production Manager: Barbara States
Production Assistant: Pat O'Maley

Printed in Hong Kong

THE AMERICAN

ARCHITECTURAL

PHOTOGRAPHER

Profiles of the Top Talent in Architectural Photography

TABLE OF CONTENTS

STEVE SIMMONS

From the time of its invention, photography has been used to describe, document, explain, and illustrate architecture to a wider audience of people than just those who could actually see the building. This primary function of photography carries on a rich tradition of drawing, painting, and etching which began in ancient times and then flourished in the 15th and 16th centuries when book production and printing became practical on a larger scale. In our modern day, the photographic image is utilized by architects in their portfolios, to enter design and awards programs, by magazines devoted to architecture, in home design, building technology, and by building materials associations to promote the use of their products.

Initially, when the photograph was used to document and record buildings, it was highly praised for its supposed ability to accurately render its subject. Photographs were not paintings or drawings whose accuracy was dependent on the skill and honesty of the artist; it was only possible to photograph what was actually there in front of the camera. Light was the only variable.

The most famous of the early architectural photographers seems to be Eugene Atget in France and Frederick Evans in England. The work of both of these photographers is classic and timeless, and has contributed greatly to our appreciation for the combination of these two forms of art. However, there were hundreds of other European photographers who worked with architecture and created wonderful images as well: Names such as Adolphe Braun, Edouard Baldus, and Gustave LeGray quickly come to mind as photographers who furthered the union of photography and architecture. The work of these early photographers was seen more as being artistic or documentary rather than commercial in the sense that we use the term today.

As photographic history moved into the early twentieth century names such as Walker Evans, (whose unforgiving views of rural Southern architecture remain with us and will for many more years), Paul Strand, Margaret Bourke-White, and Berenice Abbott come to mind as photographers whose work with architectural subjects helped make them and their subjects immortal.

The field of commercial architectural photography seems to have begun, barely, in the 1930s but to have flourished since World War II. Building and magazine publication also boomed, and this twin movement is probably responsible for much of the growth of and demand for good, commercial, architectural photographs. It is during this time that the important figures in American architectural photography begin to show themselves to the world. On the East Coast it was Ezra Stoller, in the Mid-West it was Ken Hedrich, and on the West Coast it was Morley Baer and Julius Shulman. It was their work up through the 1960s and early '70s that established the standards of the profession and whose work much of the younger photographers were measured against.

Now looking back through the 1970s and '80s one can see almost an explosion of the need for and the number of architectural photographers. Somewhere along the line the architects and others in the building and design professions discovered photography as a selling tool. This is quite different than using photography as a method of education and documentation. The switch from black and white to color in the early '70s may have harkened this change in attitude.

Magazines were quick to move from the elegant black and white image to the more seductive color reproductions. Coincidentally with the greater use of color in photography came important changes in the design of buildings and interior spaces.

With the move from Bauhaus to Post-Modern, architecture and interior design became the subject of popular demand, and the number of publications devoted to these professions, (yet really aimed at the masses for readership), increased tremendously. The need for photographers increased geometrically, as did the number of photographs.

The profession of architectural photography is now facing tremendous pressures from inside the profession as well as from the outside. The role of photography as a selling tool is being questioned by those who challenge its ability to accurately portray a building. Some have likened the use of a single photograph to illustrate a building as lifting a quote from an article. Neither of them give a complete picture of the whole piece. Even assembling several quotes from a speech, or several photographs of the same building, does not, in the eye of some, accurately communicate the complete experience of the work. Left out of the photograph, or photographs, is a sense of smell, touch, scale experienced on a personal level, and sound. The American Institute of Architects is beginning to use video as a tool to show architecture and the use of computers, 3D drawings, and virtual reality, all of which are now beginning to threaten the dominance of the still photograph as a means to show architecture. There are even those who are predicting the death of the printed publication and the increasing use of CD ROMs and computer information systems as a means for the public to obtain information about subjects that they are now accustomed to reading about in magazines.

From inside the profession of architectural photography there are pressures as well. The need for us is shrinking at a time when the number of photographers has been increasing. Competition for jobs is fierce and working conditions have become more difficult. Fees for this work have actually decreased in many areas of the country. Copyright protection, something photographers have fought for for many years is now being informally given up by many photographers just to get the chance to work. Magazines are using competitions and awards programs to generate editorial material which does not have to be paid for as the entrants, and their photographers, are asked to sign away their rights for subsequent payment upon publication as a requirement for entry into the program.

The increasing potential and use of digital imaging techniques also call into question the accuracy of photography. Some publications are quietly using this methodology to create subtle, and editorially more appropriate, photographs. Many photographers are actively exploring the use of the computer to manipulate their photographs as well — sometimes to correct photographic mistakes such as incorrect color balance, and other times to alter features of the buildings or its surroundings to make the building more attractive. While the use of this technology will undoubtedly race ahead of ethical considerations, it will only further the questioning of the accuracy and trustworthiness of the photograph as a means to communicate and describe an architectural subject. However, a restrained yet competent use of this new technology can be a great asset to the architectural photographer who can now offer new services to his/her clients.

Internal and external pressures notwithstanding, the need for still architectural photographers will continue. Magazines cannot publish videos on their pages and architects cannot hang movies on their office walls. The AIA seems committed to continuing its awards programs which will continue to use still photographs. In fact, the AIA is now going to ask that all entrants agree not to use any computer manipulations of the images thus ensuring the credibility of the accompanying photographs and the importance of a trained photographic eye. This is a real plus for the dedicated architectural photographer and indicates a strong future for the still, unmanipulated photograph.

Photographers working in this field should look back and be proud of their heritage and the importance of their own work. It is through the use of their photographs that a wider audience has been able to develop a deeper appreciation of the built environment.

Peter Aaron
Esto Photographics
222 Valley Place
Mamaroneck, NY 10543
914.698.4060
Fax: 914.698.1033

**Whittle
Communications**
Knoxville, TN
Architects
Peter Marino & Associate

PETER AARON

Peter Aaron is one of the foremost photographers of architecture and interior design. Aaron understands light and controls it to define space in extraordinary ways.

Peter Aaron's photographs create a dialogue with the viewer about action taking place in the space. Aaron's photographs have a liveliness that has become his trademark. His are identifiable images like no others.

Peter Aaron is represented by Esto which helps arrange assignments and maintains a valuable library of photographs for architects and publishers.

Whittle Communications
Knoxville, TN
Architects
Peter Marino & Associates

**Susan and Elihu Rose Suite,
The Juilliard School**
New York, NY
Architects
Davis Brody & Associates

**Walter Reade Theater,
The Film Society
of Lincoln Center**
New York, NY
Architects
David Brody & Associates

Team Disney Building
Orlando, FL
Architects
Arata Isosaki & Associates
Associate Architects
Hunton Brady Pryor Maso

PETER AARON

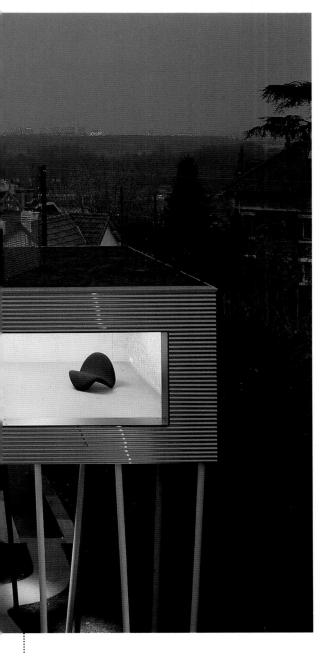

Villa Dall'Ava
St. Cloud, France
Architects
Rem Koolhaas
Xavier De Geyter
Jeroen Thomas
Office for Metropolitan Architecture

Ohrstrom Library, St. Paul's School
Concord, NH
Architect
Robert A. M. Stern

Architect
HL2L Architects/Planner

Architect
Voith & Mactavish Architects

Architect
MGA Partners

TOM BERNARD

Tom Bernard has been pursuing architectural photography since 1975 when he began his career with the firm Venturi, Rauch and Scott Brown. In 1985 he established his own firm, Tom Bernard Photography.

Tom seeks to achieve images which meet specific goals and are visually rewarding. He is particularly concerned with the quality of light, the physical context of the project and the translation of a given project's characteristics through photography. Tom encourages a close collaborative interaction with his clients which translates into a strong working relationship.

Tom has photographed projects regionally and nationally. His images have appeared in a wide range of national and international publications, and have helped his clients win numerous awards.

Client
*Adams-Bickel
Associates, Inc.*

Architects
*(A) Venturi, Rauch & Scott Brown, (B) Edwin Bronstein, AIA,
(C) Geddes Brecher Qualls Cunningham, (D) Kieran Timberlake & Harris*
Client
(E) Le Moniteur

Tom Bernard

Architect
Steve Izenour;
Venturi Scott Brown
& Associates

Architect
Susan Maxman, Architects

Architect
Steinberg and
Stevens Architects

Architect
Lyman S.A. Perry, Architect

Architect
*Cassway.Albert
& Associates*

Client
*Trump's Taj Mahal
Casino Resort*

**Mural Project
Clients**
*Meritor Bank
Corporation
and
Ueland Junker
McCauley Architects*

Architect
*Tony Atkin &
Associates, Architects*

ARCADIA PHOTOGRAPHICS, INC.
1249 PORTAGE STREET
KALAMAZOO, MI 49001
616.385.0037
FAX: 616.385.5993

Historical District
Kalamazoo

Clients

Barton Malow Co.

BCI

James E. Childs & Assoc.

The CSM Group

Daniels and Zermack Assoc.

Design Plus P.C.

DeWinter Craig

Diekema Hamann Architects

Eckert Wordell Architects

First of America Bank Corp.

Greiner, Inc.

Kingscott Associates Inc.

Luckenbach Ziegleman

Progressive AEP

Quinn Evans Architects

Jon Stryker Design

Stryker Instruments

Tower Pinkster Titus

The Upjohn Company

Wigen Tincknell Meyer

Corporate Headquarters
John E. Fetzer Institute

Gerald R. Ford Museum

20

GARY CIALDELLA

ARCADIA PHOTOGRAPHICS, INC.

A photographer for sixteen years, Gary Cialdella has specialized in architectural photography for the past six. Cialdella holds a Master of Fine Arts degree from the University of Notre Dame and has received numerous awards for his fine art photographs. His work has been widely exhibited in many locations, including the Art Institute of Chicago, and he has been published in the quarterly Aperture. Cialdella's architectural interiors emphasize controlled sculptural lighting and the formal elements of composition which work to draw the viewer into the environment.

In 1987, along with photographer Susan Carr, they formed Arcadia Photographics. Arcadia Photographics is a collaborative venture of the architectural photography of Mr. Cialdella and the still life imagery of Ms. Carr. Together they have established a studio that is known for both the creativity of their work and the quality of service they provide to their clients. Home base for Arcadia is a restored 1903 fire station in Kalamazoo, Michigan, halfway between Detroit and Chicago.

**Lobby
Biggs/Gilmore
Advertising Agency**

**Corridor
Computer Center
Holland Middle School**

GARY CIALDELLA / ARCADIA PHOTOGRAPHICS, INC.

Egypt Valley Country Club

**Media Center
Pinewood School**

Private Residence

ARCADIA PHOTOGRAPHICS, INC. / GARY CIALDELLA

Private Residence

**Library
Borgess Medical Center**

**Boardroom
Haworth, Inc.**

CARLOS DOMENECH PHOTOGRAPHY
MIAMI, FLORIDA
305.666.6964
FAX: 305.666.6964

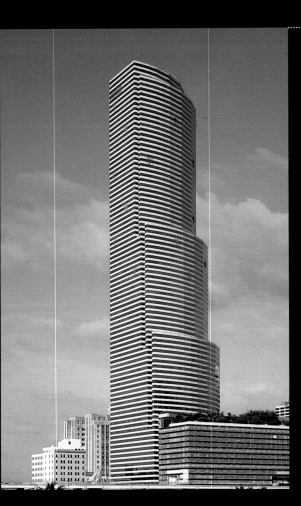

Centrust Tower
Miami, FL
Architect
I.M. Pei

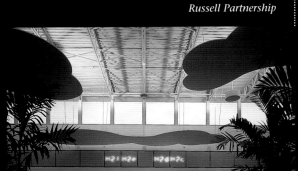

U.S. Air Terminal
Miami, FL
Architect
Russell Partnership

Publications

Antiques

Architectural Digest

Audio Video Interiors

Casa Vogue

Designers' Journal
(England)

Designers West

Florida Architect

Florida Architecture

Florida Home Garden

Garden Design

Home

House & Garden

Interiors

Progressive
Architecture

Restaurant & Hotel
Design

Southern Accents

Veranda

Ruskin Manufacturing
Hollywood, FL

"The art of documenting is no longer the most important preoccupation when photographing architecture, the art of seeing and discovering new possibilities is an equally important attribute. But overall, representing with accuracy and truth is the main objective."

Carlos Domenech is a graduate of Rochester Institute of Technology, and holds a bachelor's degree in fine art photography with a minor in architectural photography.

Based in Miami, Florida since 1983.

Tokyo Rose Restaurant
Miami, FL
Architect
Mateo/Rizo Architects

**Southern Accents
Magazine**
Hobe Sound, FL

25

Sol-Hotel
Miami Beach, FL
Designers
P.M. Corporate

RON FORTH PHOTOGRAPHY
1507 DANA AVENUE
CINCINNATI, OH 45207
513.841.0858
FAX: 513.841.0858

Cincinnati Microwave
ESCORT Store
Architect:
Michael Schuster Associates

Hardy Holzman Pfeiffer
Conference Room
Personal Work

Union Central
Life Insurance
Board Room Lobby
Client: Wall Options, Inc.

Clients

Prudential Properties

Coldwell Banker

Formica Corp.

Duke & Associates

KZF Inc.

Michael Schuster &
Associates

Leers, Weinzapfel
Associates

Eisenman Architects

A.M. Kinney
Associates

Fluor Daniel Inc.

Kajima International

Space Design
International

Arthur Schuster, Inc.

Glaser & Associates

VNA/PDT Interiors
Group

Keroff & Rosenberg

Schumacher/Dugan
Inc.

Universal Contracting
Corp.

Rubloff

Champlin-Haupt

GBBN, Inc.

Shayman & Salk Co.

Tipton Associates, Inc.

Publications

Architectural Lighting

Fine Wood Working

Design Solutions

Cincinnati Magazine

AWI Magazine

Visual Merchandising
& Store Displays

Progressive
Architecture

Historic Preservation

Architecture Magazine

Better Homes &
Gardens

Inland Architect

Builder Magazine

Professional Builder

RON FORTH

In the early 1970's, Ron Forth earned a degree in Fine Arts Photography at Ohio University. He invested much time studying the works of great photographers and artists, learning to appreciate what makes each unique in their own right.

Today, Forth again looks for the unique in every project he is assigned. Clients welcome his ability to recognize and appreciate their own design and to record it in his own unique, yet comprehensible manner. In his own words, Forth explains his penchant for his craft, "I find having to work within the limitations of the elements of nature and the mix of different lighting sources results in the most challenging type of photography."

Seven Hill Middle School
Architecture Magazine
Architects: Pellecchia Olson

CG&E Building
*Client: A.M. Kinney
Associates*

Seven Hills Middle School
Architecture Magazine
Architects: Pellechia Olson

Northside Middle School
Architecture Magazine
*Architects: Leers, Weinzapfel
Associates*

Hawkins Residence
Inland Architect
Architect: David L. Niland

Bennet Residence
Architect: Michael Schuster Associates

FINIS Lobby
Architect: Jean Cecil Gilliam, Inc.

FRANZEN PHOTOGRAPHY
145 HEKILI STREET, SUITE 100
KAILUA, HI
808.261.9998
FAX: 808.262.4456

The Lodge at Koele,
Lanai, Hawaii
Group 70, 1990

Sheraton Palace Hotel,
San Francisco, CA
Hideto Horiike Architects

Clients
HKS, Inc.
Ellerbe Becket
Hideto Horiike & Assoc
Group 70
Winberly Allison Tong
& Goo
Gwathmey Siegel
Bechtel International
William Turnbull
Phillip Johnson
Kajima Associates
ABB Power Generation
Gulstrom Kosko
DMJM
John Hara & Assoc.
Fletcher Pacific

Publications
AIA Journal
Architectural Record
Interiors
House Beautiful

Restaurant, Honolulu
Gulstrom Kosko, 1990

Photographs © David Franzen

DAVID FRANZEN

David Franzen has been photographing award winning architecture and interiors for 20 years. His clients are architects, interior designers, developers, engineers and corporations. David's photographs have been published extensively both nationally and internationally.

Advertisement for Fletcher Pacific, 1992

David Franzen

Honolulu Residence
Gulstrom Kosko, 1990

Residential bath, Honolulu
Real estate Advertisement,
1992

Uraku Tower Lobby, Honolulu
Kajima & Associates, 1991

Honolulu Apartment
Merrill & Associates, 1989

Alii Tower, Honolulu
DMJM Hawaii, 1993

JONATHAN HILLYER PHOTOGRAPHY, INC.
2604 PARKSIDE DRIVE, N.E.
ATLANTA, GA 30305
404.841.6679
FAX: 404.841.9088

Residence
Baltimore, MD

Clients
Allied/Signal

BASF

Burlington Industries

E.I. du Pont de
Nemours

Graham Gund
Architects

Interface Flooring
Systems

Jova Daniels Busby

Lockwood Greene

Lord, Aeck & Sargent

Pryor & Morrow
Architects

Shaw Industries

The Design Company

The Knoll Group

Publications
Architectural Record

Architecture

Architectur &
Wettbewerbe

L'Industria Della
Costruzioni

Interior Design

Progressive
Architecture

Southern Accents

103 West
Atlanta, GA

**Southern Progress
Corporation**
Birmingham, AL

**Sonoco Products
Company**
Hartsville, SC

JONATHAN HILLYER

Jonathan Hillyer graduated from Rhode Island School of Design and has been working with architects, interior designers, and corporate clients for 16 years.

Perspective, composition, and light powerfully capture the essence of architectural structure as well as the intimacy of thought behind design detail. Fleeting light is often the expression which metamorphoses the three-dimensional subject into the richness of Mr. Hillyer's photographic work.

It is his commitment to collaboration and his alliance with his clients which coaxes the sensitive balance of interpretation. Jonathan Hillyer continues to create important images for major international architectural, and interior design firms as well as furniture, interior accessories, carpeting and textiles.

The Trinity School
Atlanta, GA

Residence
North Georgia

**JONATHAN HILLYER
PHOTOGRAPHY, INC.
2604 PARKSIDE DRIVE, N.E.
ATLANTA, GA 30305
404.841.6679
FAX: 404.841.9088**

**Fuller E. Callaway Manufacturing
Research Center at Georgia Institute of Technology**
Atlanta, GA

**Delta Airlines Reservations
and Training Center**
Salt Lake City, UT

**Fernbank Museum of
Natural History**
Atlanta, GA

HOACHLANDER PHOTOGRAPHY ASSOCIATES
903 GIRARD STREET NE
WASHINGTON, DC 20017
202.832.4870
FAX: 202.832.0298

Detail of the Tycon Courthouse lobby
Falls Church, , VA
Client
Heery International, Inc.

The employee cafeteria at the
U.S. Department of the Treasury
Washington, D.C.
Client
Cooper-Lecky Architects, P.C.

The VIP/Green room
at Atlantic Video
Washington, D.C.
Client
The Weihe Partnership

Clients

Hellmuth Obata &
Kassabaum, Inc.

Heery International,
Inc.

Pennsylvania Avenue
Development Corp.

DIFFA

Trammel Crow
Company

Sigal Construction

The Weihe Partnership

National Trust for
Historic Preservation

Centermark
Properties, Inc.

U.S. Department of
the Treasury

National Building
Museum

Publications

Inform

Mid-Atlantic Country

Hospitality Design

Casabella

Progressive
Architecture

Architectural Record

Interior Design

Historic Preservation

Baltimore Magazine

Historic Preservation
News

Washington Post

ANICE HOACHLANDER

Anice Hoachlander has specialized in architectural photography for over a decade. Her work has been internationally published, utilized in large scale documentary projects and showcased in commercial portfolios and brochures. Ms. Hoachlander is an expert in interior photographic lighting techniques, and is proficient with all types of lighting equipment essential to insuring correct color rendition and clarity of detail. In her approach to exterior work, she takes utmost care in making use of variable light and weather conditions to enhance the design elements of the architecture.

Hoachlander Photography Associates is an award winning studio based in Washington D.C., which concentrates primarily upon the commercial, historical, and archival documentation of architecture and interior design. Dedicated to meeting the needs of clients during all phases of design and development, the studio also offers model documentation and scaled elevation photography that can be transferred directly to working drawings.

The ruins of Rosewell Mansion
Gloucester, VA
Client
The Rosewell Foundation

A residence on Spa Creek
Annapolis, MD
Client
Design Dwelling

ANICE HOACHLANDER

**The entrance of the
Tycon Courthouse lobby**
Falls Church, VA
Client
Heery International, Inc.

**The School of Architecture
at Catholic University
of America**
Washington D.C.
Client
Catholic University

The employee cafeteria at Atlantic Video
Washington D.C.
Client
The Weihe Partnership

Interior of the
Francois-Xavier Bagnoud house
Washington, D.C.
Client
DIFFA

**Interior detail of a
residence in Bayhead**
Martha's Vineyard, MA
Client
Brenda Sanchez Architects

**An exterior detail of a
residence in Bayhead**
Martha's Vineyard, MA
Client
Brenda Sanchez Architects

STEVE ROSENTHAL

THE EYE OF AN ARCHITECT

How long have you been an architectural photographer?

I started in '71 so that's 18 years or so. I started out as an architect. I went to architecture school at Harvard University and then worked for four years at the Cambridge Seven Associates Group, an architectural firm. I did a lot of in-house photography — 35mm photography of buildings and models.

I made the career change because I thought I worked better translating three dimensions into two rather than the two into three which is your task in designing a building. I just feel more comfortable and better at it (photography) than I would have been as an architect.

Do you think that your training as an architect helps you?

No doubt about it. It really gives you an intuitive understanding of space, and I think it helps me understand the way architects think about their work and understand the way they like to see their work presented. I also tend to see the flaws in their work more readily than a layman would. It puts you on the same wave length as architects. I can understand what they are thinking and talk their language. Every profession has it's jargon. I like architects, and that has nothing to do with having been one or being one (I still am an architect). I just think they are decent, honest people and pleasant people to work for. They're gentlemen and don't try to take advantage of you. I can't say that about everybody who's involved in the building process. Architects also understand and respect the creative process.

How much do you work and how often do you shoot?

Recently I have been trying to cut back on working evenings, trying not to be in the darkroom. For years and years I was doing all the darkroom printing and developing all the black and white negatives. With shooting in the day time and printing at night and I'd be working until midnight every night. That's a prescription for burn-out. I've been trying to keep more control of it and delegating more of it to other people, so I don't do any printing anymore if I can help it. Basically, we have other people doing all of that stuff although we do everything in-house except dupes. I'm doing the shooting, and I'm still doing a lot of phone calls and overseeing the business. I'll shoot Saturday this weekend, and I shot last Sunday, but only when forced into it by weather conditions.

What about camera movements in architectural photography? Which ones do you use the most?

Rise and fall and shift. I really don't use the swing and tilts too much.

What about swings on the back?

I don't use that very much either. I use it sometimes, but not that much. Do you use it much?

No, but I use it at times when I have to look at things more obliquely than I want to. I will swing the back to square things up a little bit.

Yes, but you have to be careful using those movements because it throws everything else off.

Who's work did you look at early in your career?

Ezra Stoller's work more than anybody else. What I call the older generation, a generation older than me. Photographers such as Stoller, Julius Shulman and Morley Baer. At that time there were only a handful of photographers doing really good work.

Did you ever assist anyone? Actually you started doing this type of work when you worked in the architect's office on your own, didn't you?

No, I was never an assistant but I have had the opportunity to watch other photographers work. I went out with Julius Shulman one day in the early 70s. I assisted him for a one day shoot of a house in Connecticut. It takes a lot of the mystique out of photography when you go out with somebody else and you find there really aren't any secrets, gimmicks or tricks out there. It's just hard work and knowing what you're doing. Everybody works differently. You end up working in ways that you know work for you, that you can rely on. People, I guess, approach things differently. They sort of come at it in a different way. It's just damn hard work.

It is a much more a physical task than I ever anticipated.

Yes, it really is. I'm tired today, just spending half a day shooting. It is strenuous work. Not only the physical aspects of it, but there's a lot of mental stress when you're working quickly; you're trying to set up lights and the sun is moving; and you've got trucks, and all sorts of obstacles there that are out of your control. Architectural photography is a medium in which one wants to have complete control. You want to be able to control the situation as much as possible, I do at least. I want to have complete control over the frame itself and the composition of the objects within the frame. When things start happening that I just don't have control over, it's very, very stressful. I haven't learned to sort of roll with the punches enough to be relaxed and say, "Oh well, we'll try to make the best of this." There are times when you really have to take this attitude.

Do you scout the building before you photograph it?

I always try to scout it ahead of time if it's close enough. If it isn't nearby, I try to get as much information about the building as I can. I obtain a packet of information on every project I shoot. I get plans, photographs, slides, site plan — whatever input I can to enable me to understand as much as I can. Then when I visit it, I mark the plan with potential views and lighting information. I mark whatever I can figure out from the plan, whatever questions there are, and the things that need attending to such as areas or detailing that aren't complete, burned out bulbs, barriers, obstacles; all the kinds of things you want to head off before you arrive to shoot. The worst scenario is to arrive at the site to shoot, the sun shining, you're ready to go, and somebody has dug up the pavement in front of the building or whatever — unanticipated kinds of things. I really want to understand the building. I want to understand what is in the architect's mind and how he/she approached the building.

What do you ask the architect?

I usually let him explain to me what the design parameters were and explain to me how the building is organized: why it's organized that way; why they used the materials they did; and how the circulation works. A lot of these things I obviously don't have to ask him, but it's always good to get the information and input on things that didn't work out. A lot of times there are things that aren't immediately obvious to anyone except someone involved in the design process – certain things that didn't get designed quite the right way or didn't get built right by the contractors. Sometimes those things stand out like a real sore thumb to the architect but aren't very obvious to someone else. These are the elements you try to avoid playing up in the photograph either by covering them up or shooting around them.

Who are your clients?

In most cases the architect is our client. There are times we're working directly for a magazine or for a developer, but basically we're working for an architect.

We like to work with people who are concerned with the environment. People who are making a good and improved environment and people who are concerned about space and the quality of that space. My background is in architecture. I like architecture, and I like working for these people.

What is your task as an architectural photographer?

I'm interested in space, in defining space and illustrating the relationship between spaces. We are trying to interpret buildings for people who haven't seen them. I think of that as a professional responsibility. The architectural profession reads magazines and that's how they know what's happening in their field. It's like a doctor who reads a medical journal to know what's going on in his field. Architects know what's going on in architecture not by visiting buildings and knowing them firsthand, but by looking at photographs of buildings. If you talk to architects and ask if they are familiar with this or that building, they'll say "yes," but if you ask if they've seen the building, they'll say "no." Architects are familiar with the photographs of the buildings rather than the building itself. The architectural photographer has a responsibility to portray and capture the spirit of the building and to make it understandable to someone who hasn't actually visited the project.

What about interior photography for interior designers. Is that a different job?

With interior design, the emphasis is really on fabrics, textures, furnishings, window treatment and on goods rather than on spatial relationships. So all those photographs are very two dimensional. They're not very spatial and a lot of times you feel there's so much stuff in the picture you could never enter the frame. Cushions and pillows and everything — which is great for advertising; these things go hand in hand.

I feel that much of the interior design photographs are done to falsify the mood of the space and are deliberately done with theatrical lighting. It's a movement that started about ten years ago, using lights in a way that really is more like theater lighting than architectural lighting or real lighting — using lights on the floor, uplighting. You look at the photographs that appear in those magazines and know the lighting could never really be that way in reality. The lighting has nothing to do with the space. It helps sell the magazines but they don't accurately describe the space.

How do you use supplemental lighting?

What we're trying to do with lighting is to compensate for the fact that the eye sees things very differently than film sees things. The film doesn't have the ability to handle the same ranges of contrast that the eye does. When I'm using lights, I am not trying to falsify the mood of the space, but trying to make the space feel the way it feels when you're there. We're obviously showing things in their best light if we're shooting architecture under the best of circumstances. Paul Goldberger, the architectural critic for the *New York Times*, described our task by saying that the architectural photographer's role is to give the building the fairest chance to speak for itself. I think that's a pretty fair description of what we're trying to do.

It takes a lot of patience to be a good architectural photographer. You have to like architecture. You have to care about it. If you don't care about it and your heart isn't in it, you just aren't going to do it well. You have to like the project. You have to try to find a way to like it. You have to find something about it that is interesting; some way of getting into liking it. You have to find a way of liking the people you are working with because that could turn you off.

When you're working with exteriors, do you work with daylight or tungsten film? Do you have a preference?

I shoot tungsten film almost exclusively. We have occasionally shot some 400 Vericolor when I need the extra speed, but generally in 4 x 5 I'm working with tungsten film inside and outside, using the 85B filter under daylight conditions. I like the quality of tungsten film and the convenience of using just one film so that I can load film for the next day and know that regardless of whether the sun is in or out, whether I'm shooting inside or outside, I've got film loaded that I'm going to be able to use.

That's one reason. The other reason is that Kodak tungsten film tends to have lower contrast than the daylight films, and I don't like the daylight films. The Vericolor Type S crosses over pretty badly when you get into longer exposures. Those films are not intended for exposures longer than 1/10th of a second. Tungsten film and an 85B filter also works well with a strobe, believe it or not. You take the Type L film and use it for short exposures such as 1/300th of a second or 1/500th of a second and a strobe, it handles it reasonably well. Sounds crazy. Lots of people don't believe it, but I've been shooting tungsten exclusively now in 4 x 5 for seven or eight years.

Do you have a preference for working with hot lights or strobes?

I prefer working with hot lights, but I do work with strobes. Most studio photographers work with strobe, but when we're photographing an architectural model in the studio, I never use a strobe because I can't really fine tune it. I can't really see what the light is doing. You have to depend on Polaroid. I'd much rather work with a light source where I can really see it. I only use strobe when I really need a lot of light, daylight color or the other things strobe can do such as stop action.

If you were photographing a house and you wanted a light, bright daytime look, would you use strobe for that or would you mask and unmask windows?

Well, usually I would use the strobe. We've done some masking of the window technique also, but that's time consuming — really time consuming. I find it's hard to stay on a schedule where I've got a certain number of pictures to do in a day, and I've got to do them at a certain time because the sun is in a certain location. Even on interiors, the position of the sun in the sky can be important. I just find the masking procedure

can get very tedious and slow unless you're talking about a few little windows which I can do rather easily. It's a great technique, but I tend not to use it very often.

Has the shift from having magazines hire photographers to having architects hiring photographers changed your job, or the demands and requirements that you have to fulfill?

Even when the magazines were hiring photographers, and the magazines still do hire photographers, it was almost always with the approval of the architect. I think the work was and still is influenced by the way the architect wants it to be seen. What I try to do is explain the building, the concept of the building. As a photographer, I am trying to see the building through the architect's eyes. We've done some retrospective stories where I've gone back and photographed a building after it's been occupied for five years. We've been hired by the magazine and the article is a critique on the way the occupant is using the building and we want to know whether the building has lived up to its expectations in every facet. I think in those cases I had more freedom to look at the building totally objectively from the user's point of view. Doing editorializing with the camera. I've really enjoyed these projects, because I felt there was a lot that could be learned from them. Often buildings get published when they're the new, hot thing and then lots of times they don't work out very well.

What changes have you seen in the profession in the last twenty-five years or so, if any?

One change would be that the emphasis has shifted, as I mentioned before, from publication to selling. Not that there isn't still a strong need and desire on the part of publications, but photographs now are being used more for promotion. There is an every day need for these pictures to go out and solicit new projects.

Also, there is tremendous change in emphasis from black and white to color. It's generated from the fact that magazines are able to run more color cheaper and that all the magazines and publications have been generally moved toward color. It's become more popular in the last fifteen years or so. When we started out, we were doing 90 percent black and white in the early 70s and about 10 percent color, and I think that was the same with the publications. No it's really flip flopped completely so that about 10 percent of the prints we do are black and white and 90 percent are color.

Does it make our job easier or tougher?

It makes it tougher in some ways because mixed light sources are something you can get away with very easily in black and white. It requires a lot of hard work when it comes to shooting color as you know. I end up having to do an awful lot of technical shenanigans just do get the color clean. When interiors have two, three, or four different kinds of light sources in it, you end up being a technician. It's very hard to still stay creative and fresh setting up a photograph, because you have so many technical constraints to deal with that the artistic side of the picture can get less energy focused on it.

I would almost prefer doing residential projects, because I don't have the mix of lighting.

Yes. You don't have the mix of lights and the spaces are small. It's really a different approach. The problem is that we end up shooting in large commercial spaces that are lit with lights that were never intended to be used in interior areas. I am talking about Sodium Vapor, Mercury Vapor, and Metal Halide bulbs. These were intended to illuminate sidewalks and parking lots at night. We're working for people who want to see true color. They've spent a lot of time selecting colors of the fabrics and paint colors on the wall. Especially now, a lot of the colors you see used in these post-modern buildings are pastel shades which are very subtle. A little bit of color cast on a pastel wall really throws it off. We're trying to portray these colors as they were selected and as they actually appear working with light sources which have an incomplete spectrum in that they are deficient in the red areas of the visible color spectrum. So we're working with our hands tied behind our backs with these kinds of sources. I feel like I want to be able to get at lighting designers and give them an education not only in terms of the way film sees these light sources, but what it feels like to be under these lights.

Does the style of the building, whether it's Modern, Post Modern, or other styles influence you on how you photograph it or how you approach the building? In terms of how you approach the forms, lighting, or anything?

One of the challenges of doing this kind of work, is to have enough flexibility to be able to see the building through the architect's eye. Really, what you're trying to do is interpret the building through the eyes of the creator. I think one has to be tolerant enough to enjoy many different approaches to architecture, not only enjoy them but to be enthusiastic about different approaches. One needs to realize that there is validity to lots of different ways of designing. I think many architects are too intolerant to do what I do, because they're very opinionated about what they do and do not like in terms of design. One of the challenges is to try to understand the building, understand what the person created, and was trying to do, and try to be sympathetic to that approach. If you don't feel you can be, you shouldn't take the job. You just shouldn't take on the assignment. One's approach should be flexible enough to allow yourself to do that. You shouldn't impose your style on the building. Everyone has style that's going to come through, but you shouldn't approach it with a lot of preconceptions about how you're going to do it until you've understood it.

So you wouldn't necessarily approach a more historical type of style any differently than you would approach something that was real modern or contemporary?

I think that's really hard to generalize. I think there are buildings that work well in their context, but when one tries to emphasize the context more, the building becomes jarring. When one is serving the architect's needs, you tend to show the building in ways that are visually successful.

Is it important to shoot the building in its context or to try and isolate it, or do you do both?

I think you should show it in its context. I think that's an obligation you have, especially in an editorial use. It's one thing if you're photographing solely for the architect.

This relates to the question asked earlier about whether it's different shooting for a magazine as opposed to shooting for the architect. I think the magazine has an obligation to show the building in it's context, because one of the magazine's purposes is to try to reach a greater audience than would otherwise be able to see the building itself. Most people don't know buildings, they know pictures of buildings which have appeared in magazines.

An architect, in photographing his building, has a different need. If it doesn't really work too well in it's context, he isn't going to want to show it because he's really looking at it in terms of sales and marketing. The recent trend, picking up on what we discussed earlier, is a lot more emphasis on selling. Instead of doing a complete story of a building so that somebody can understand it through the photographs and understand how the spaces relate to each other there's been more emphasis, both in the magazine and with architect's, in getting a few catchy photographs, sexy photographs of something that is eyecatching. I feel the magazines are guilty of that too because their number of pages are down, and they are not able to concentrate on a building with six or eight pages any longer. There are just one, two or four pages on many of the buildings. Four pages is good coverage these days. They're just showing bits and pieces of the building instead of showing enough photographs to completely illustrate the building, its setting and design. I think that's frustrating because it tends to make the articles on the buildings and our work more superficial. I used to think that what we did made it possible for somebody to understand the building through the photographs.

The reader should be able to visualize a sequence of movement through a building by using the photographs so that they can understand, really understand the building. Understand each space and understand how the spaces relate to each other. But, things are changing.

So there is more emphasis on selling now. Does that mean there is more emphasis on glamorizing the building beyond what it deserves? Is there more of a push for the photographer to glamorize the building than maybe 20 or 25 years ago?

There is a lot of glamorizing done, especially in interiors. I think there's been a lot of that going on, and it's been fed by some of the interiors magazines which have really ended up with photographs that are fabrications. They're theatrical stage sets. The lighting has no relationship to the lighting that actually exists. Strobes give an awful lot of potential for dishonesty. Because they're so powerful, you can completely overwhelm the feeling of the space. You can completely change the character of lighting in a space with strobes; make light appear to come from a direction where there are no windows. You can do things with lighting that are very dramatic. You've seen this whole school of photography where you get lights on the floor and shadows on the ceiling — uplighting. This movement has been fueled by a group of people who were doing photographs for the interior-oriented publications. They are very dramatic, very splashy but they are not photographs of space, but of the objects in the room. Rarely do you see a ceiling and if it is shown it's played down by throwing a light up through some plants that casts shadows on the ceiling. To me, it's a falsification, but it does sell magazines and advertising.

Does this same kind of photography show up in the architectural magazines and work done for architects?

I guess I keep coming back to that question of the difference between working for magazines versus working for architects. Magazines are interested in selling magazines, especially the ones that are so called "shelter" magazines, but the architect knows that if he falsifies the feel of his space too much, there's always going to be a selection committee or somebody who's going to come through and actually see the building. If the architect makes it to the short list to be selected to do the project, I think people will look at the photographs a lot more skeptically when they realize that the photograph has very little relationship to the final product. I think in those cases, it's doing the architect a dis-service to present photographs that distort the character of an interior space to that extent. We're really trying to capture the essence of an interior. We move things around, of course, but only to make the space work for the photograph.

What's two feet out of the photograph doesn't enter into your experience at all, whereas when you're standing in a space, what's all around you is part of your experience. The camera is in one place and has only a narrow view. One has to find that one spot that optimizes all the relationships and then try to introduce the feeling of what is behind the camera and out-side of the view into that frame. There are times when you are accused of being dishonest for changing things in the photograph from the way they are in reality, but in fact, what you're trying to do is capture the feeling and spirit of the space by introducing things that are outside of the frame to give it the feel that it needs to do justice to the picture. I'm not talking about falsifying, but about introducing things into the photograph that emphasize the spirit of the place.

A good example of this is a photograph we did for the Harvard Club. There's a lot of memorabilia on the walls of the Harvard Club, but much of it was outside of the frame of the photograph the way the particular camera location was being set up. So what we did was take photographs down from the walls all around us and placed them within the photograph. I guess some people would say we were distorting the space and not showing it the way it is. But really, in a way I think we were being more honest to the space. What we were trying to do was introduce things that you know are there when you're standing there but don't happen to be in the picture. There's a lot of subjectivity that goes into the process.

How do you handle the business aspects of the profession? Do you maintain rights to your photographs or does the client own the images?

I try to go along with what I consider to be the generally accepted practices of architectural photography. Generally, we work this way with almost everybody: we work for our clients at a day rate which allows them to use the photographs for their own promotional purposes and for promoting themselves with the potential client. This means they can use them for proposals, award programs, slide shows, submission to magazines, but it does not include the right for the magazine to use the material. We retain publication rights for magazine use. We retain advertising use and all third party usage.

There's no reason why the architect should subsidize everybody else's use of the photographs. So the arrangement that has evolved over the years is that the architect gets the pictures at a lower rate than it would cost him if he were paying a regular commercial studio rate in this city or any other city. But in exchange, the photographer retains a lot more rights and has a lot more potential for rights than he would otherwise.

The architect doesn't want to be in the business of selling uses. They prefer all of those requests from third parties go through the photographer and we do charge a usage fee to third parties. That's the way we work and that's the way most architectural photographers work with an architect.

Reprinted with permission from **View Camera** *magazine.*

TIMOTHY HURSLEY

TIMOTHY HURSLEY

The Renaissance Center
Detroit, MI
Architect
John Portman

The Corning Glass Factory
This building has been destroyed.

Abandoned Steel Mill
Birmingham, AL

TIMOTHY HURSLEY

**The National
Gallery of Canada**
by Moshe Safdie

**Brothel Interior —
Chicken Ranch**
Parumph, NV

**Brothel Interior,
Conforte Suite —
Mustang Ranch**
Reno, NV

TIMOTHY HURSLEY

Philip Johnson's Study

The Mariott Apartment
by Krueck & Olsen (now Krueck & Sexton)
Chicago, IL

JEFFREY JACOBS
MIMSTUDIOS
2258 YOUNG AVENUE
MEMPHIS, TN 38104
901.725.4040
FAX: 901.725.7643

Clients

Holiday Inn World Wide

Peachtree Windows & Doors

Federal Express

Turner Construction

Trammell Crow

Boyle Investment Co.

Belz Enterprises

Archer/Malmo Advertising

Windsor Properties

I.D.I.

H.D.R. Omaha Office

Rosser FABRAP International- Atlanta Office

Publications

Architecture

Better Homes & Gardens

Modern Steel Construction

Builder Magazine

Decorating and Remodeling

House & Garden

Interior Construction

Professional Photographer

Professional Builder & Remodeler

The Allenburg Building
Memphis, TN
Architects
*Hnedak Bobo Group
Architects
Memphis, TN*

JEFFREY JACOBS

Dedicated to the artful expression of architectural form in photography. Understanding the art of architecture is the first step in capturing the feel of a space. Expressing that form in photographic composition is the goal of Jeffrey Jacobs. His dedication to architectural expression shows through in years of outstanding work for architects, publications and advertising clients.

Technical excellence with attention to critical detail.
From the simplest interiors to massive spaces, Jacobs understands the nuances of detailing. Special lighting considerations, to capture the layering of space and the tectonics of detail, are familiar and welcome challenges.

Reliable. Professional.
Years of experience and his pride in a beautiful image has given Jacobs' clients results that often exceed their expectations. His consistency in providing these images with attention to critical deadlines has established long term working relationships with national corporations and publications, architects, and advertising agencies.

Fulton County Government Center
Atlanta, GA
Architects
Turner/FABRAP (joint venture) – Atlanta, GA

Jeffrey Jacobs

Palmer Residence
Memphis, TN
Architects
*Looney, Ricks, Kiss
Architects
L.R.K. Interiors
Memphis, TN*

**Children's Museum
of Memphis**
Memphis, TN
Exhibit Design
*Williamson/Haizlip
Memphis, TN*

**Rooney-Brenner
Residence**
Memphis, TN
Architects
*Looney, Ricks, Kiss
Architects
Memphis, TN*

Private Residence
Oxford, MS
Architects
*Mockbee, Coker
Jackson, MS*

THOMAS K. LEIGHTON
321 EAST 43RD STREET
PENTHOUSE #12
NEW YORK, NY 10017
212.370.1835

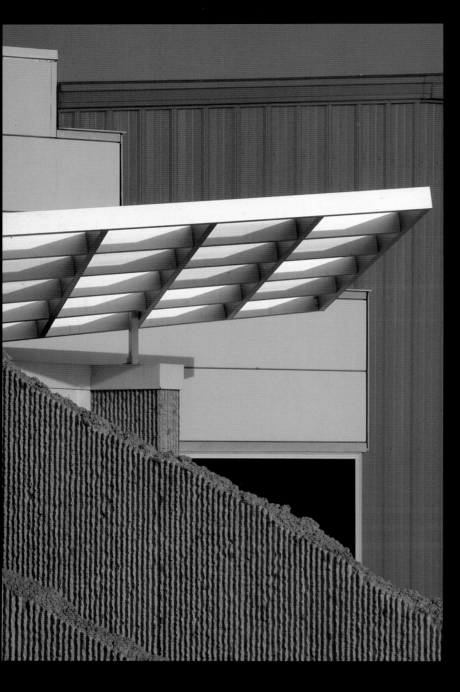

Thomas K. Leighton

Working primarily in the 35mm format, Tom Leighton specializes in architectural and interior photography with an emphasis on color and graphics. His bold images convey a strong sense of personal involvement in the representation of his subjects. Tom's photography makes use of eye-catching angles and a keen sense of light to create unique and striking images.

MAXWELL MACKENZIE
2641 GARFIELD STREET, NW
WASHINGTON, DC 20008
202.232.6686
FAX: 202.232.6684

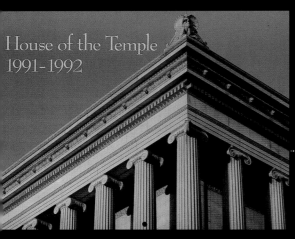

House of the Temple
1991-1992

The Fashion Centre at Pentagon City
Arlington, VA
Architect
RTKL Associates
Developer
Melvin Simon & Assoc.

Regardie's Luxury Homes, Washington, 1989
Belgian Embassy, which is a 1931 reproduction of the Hotel de Charolais in Paris, built in 1700.
Architect
Horace Trumbauer

1991-1992 "House of the Temple" Calendar, Cover
One in a series for the Supreme Council 33rd degree, A&ASR of Freemasonry, Washington, DC
Architect
John Russell Pope

Clients
Bell Atlantic
Boston Properties
Four Seasons Hotels
HOK
IBM
IKEA
Kodak
3M
Mobil
Perkins & Will
Sheraton Hotels
Skidmore, Owings & Merrill
The Architects Collaborative
Westin Hotels

Publications
Architectural Record
Architecture
Interior Design
Interiors
Progressive Architecture
Southern Accents

Evert Township Schoolhouse
Battle Lake, MN (From the Otter Tail County Series, a work in progress.)

MAXWELL MACKENZIE

Maxwell MacKenzie began his photographic career in an old coffee warehouse on the Thames in Wapping, East London, shooting ads and editorial work in England, France, Greece, Mauritius and Morocco. In 1981 he moved his base to Washington, D.C. to take advantage of the emerging real estate boom and began working with the developers, architects and interior designers prospering there. "Beauty" shots of commercial and residential exteriors were in great demand, but MacKenzie found he also enjoyed shooting interiors, which now account for much of his practice."... There are many technical problems to overcome, but there are also more factors under your control. You can really transform the space with your lighting if given enough time, and that's very satisfying."

MacKenzie's assignments have taken him up and down the East coast, West to Dallas and Chicago, and over seas to the Bahamas and Brazil. He recently began work on a book project, using a panoramic camera to focus on the landscapes and simple pioneer structures of his native northern Minnesota, a selection from which is scheduled for exhibition in 1993 at the AIA Headquarters in Washington.

Jenner & Block Law Offices
Washington, DC
Architect
Oldham & Seltz

Architecture Magazine
April, 1991
2401 Pennsylvania Avenue
Washington, DC
Architect
Florance Eichbaum
Esocoff King

Hugo Boss shop
Chevy Chase, MD
Architect
Salo Levinas
Owner
Alain Chetrit

Maxwell MacKenzie

Daly World newsletter
*National Conference of
Catholic Bishops/U.S.
Catholic Conference*
Architect
Leo A. Daly

Veranda Magazine
*Reprint featuring a
private apartment in
Chevy Chase, MD.*
Designer
Mary Drysdale

Veranda Magazine
*Spread featuring a
private apartment in
Washington, DC.*
Designer
Mary Drysdale

American Center
Tysons Corner, VA
Client
*Metropolitan Life
International Real Estate*

RTKL newsletter
Fall, 1992
IBM/Kodak facility
near Rochester, NY
Architect
RTKL Associates

**The George
Washington University/
VIrginia Campus**
Ashburn, VA
Architect
*Florance Eichbaum
Esocoff King*

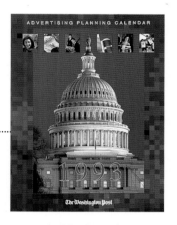

The Washington Post
*Advertising calendar
featuring the West Front
of the U.S. Capitol
Dome at dusk.*

**"STENDIG" Showroom
at The Washington
Design Center**
Washington, DC
Client
Sigal Construction Co.

Identity, Fall 1992
*Featuring Reston
Town Center, VA*
Architect
RTKL Associates
Planner
Sasaki Associates

NORMAN McGRATH, PHOTOGRAPHER
164 WEST 79TH STREET
NEW YORK, NY 10024
FON: 212.799.6422
FAX: 212.799.1285

Bank Polska
Alan Youkel, Architect

Clients

Architectural Digest

Bulgari

Carlyle Hotel

Centerbrook Architects

Chermayeff & Geismar

Connaissance des Arts

GBQC Architects

Gwathmey/Siegel

Hard Rock Cafe

Hardy Holzman Pfeiffer

Helpern Architects

Philip Johnson

McDonald's Corporation

Metropolitan Museum of Art

Museum of Television & Radio

Planet Hollywood

Prentice & Chan, Ohlhausen

Sotheby's

Spillis Candela & Partners

Stroheim & Romann

USG Corporation

Whisler-Patri

NORMAN McGRATH

Norman McGrath offers top quality photography of architecture, interior design, products, and personnel for all your promotional needs: Advertising, Brochure, Catalogue, Editorial, and Portfolio. Critically acclaimed and widely published in the US and abroad, Norman McGrath provides the expertise and experience that products and designs of quality deserve.

Photographing Buildings Inside and Out, by Norman McGrath, has become the standard reference publication in the field for both architects and photographers. The 1993 revised and updated edition is now available.

Norman McGrath teaches at both the Maine and Palm Beach Photographic Workshops.

Planet Hollywood
New York City

Sculpture Pavilion
Philip Johnson, Architect

Library
Stella Waitzkin

NORMAN McGRATH

Kawamata Project
Roosevelt Island

Tadashi Kawamata

Cohen Apartment
Room Service Design

HARRISON NORTHCUTT
ARCHITECTURAL PHOTOGRAPHY
400 F WOODCHASE LANE
MARIETTA, GA 30067
404.980.0072
FAX: 404.980.0947

**Holliday, Couch,
Hollis, and Jelks, AIA**
*Pediatric intensive care unit
at the Medical Center of
Central Georgia*

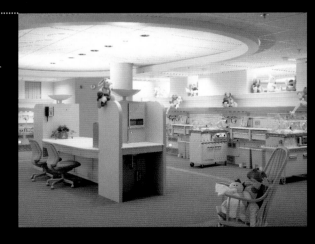

**Hollis, Jelks and
McLees, AIA**
*Women's Services Family
Birth Center at the Medical
Center of Central Georgia*

Clients

American Desk
Manufacturing Co.

Beers Construction
Company

Bellsouth

Cherry, Roberts &
Associates, AIA

Danielson and Paine,
AIA

Dorsett Carpet

Eagle Windows and
Doors, Inc.

Florist Transworld
Delivery (FTD)

Georgia World
Congress Center

Hill Rom, Inc.

Holder Construction
Company

Hollis, Jelks, &
McLees, AIA

H. Robertson, Inc.

Lyman & Davidson,
AIA

Morton International,
Inc.

P.A. Dangar
Construction Co.

Sides & Pope, AIA

Smallwood, Reynolds,
Stewart, Stewart, AIA

Southern Staircase

Stanley, Love-Stanley,
AIA

Harrison
NORTHCUTT
ARCHITECTURAL PHOTOGRAPHY

Represented By: Sullivan & Associates   3805 Maple Court, Marietta, Georgia 30066   404/971 6782   Fax: 404/973 3331

HARRISON NORTHCUTT

A native of Birmingham, Alabama, Harrison Northcutt is an Architectural photographer based in Atlanta, Georgia. He is represented in the Southeast by Sullivan & Associates. Harrison's formal education includes a B.A. Degree in Commercial Photography from Brooks Institute of Photography, Santa Barbara, California, as well as a B.S. Degree in Marketing from Auburn University, Auburn, Alabama.

Harrison's affiliation with professional associations include American Institute of Architects (AIA) and American Society of Magazine Photographers (ASMP). He has had many articles published relating to business and photography and occasionally has been quoted in national publications like Time magazine. Harrison's work has also been published in coffee table books such as ASMP's Ten Thousand Eyes (an international book project in which only 162 out of over 5,000 photographers were selected), African American Architects and The Big Click: Photographing Georgia July 2-5, 1992.

Harrison is primarily a location photographer and produces photography that has the look and feel of a natural setting. He is highly proficient in working with "available light" while also using supplemental 'fill lighting" when needed. Harrison's ability to understand and accommodate the client's needs keep him in demand, especially in difficult situations such as shoots with mixed light sources or nearly impossible time constraints. His business and marketing knowledge, coupled with a strong technical expertise in photography, allows him to work effectively with architects as well as agency, publication, and corporate clients.

American Desk Manufacturing Company, Public Seating Division
Photograph for use in corporate marketing literature.

"The Big Click: Photographing Georgia, July 2-5, 1992"
Photograph for book cover and opening spread.

Georgia Dome/Atlanta Falcons Stadium
A twilight image used by the Georgia World Congress Center for the cover of a public relations brochure.

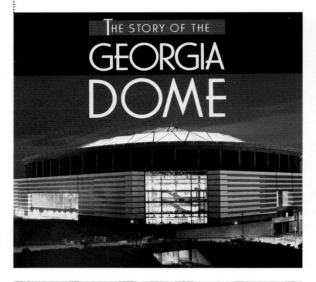

Worthington Group, Inc.
Photograph for brochure showcasing up-scale architectural products.

Dining Out in Atlanta
Cover photograph for a annual restaurant connoisseur's guide.

American Society of Magazine Photographers (ASMP)
Originally photographed for use as a postcard by the Metropolitan Theaters Corporation.

JMB Properties
Cover photograph of Southlake Mall, Atlanta, GA for a commercial real estate marketing brochure.

Eagle Windows and Doors
Photograph for use in a corporate marketing brochure.

Lyman & Davidson, A.I.A.
Photograph for architectural portfolio and marketing literature

ERIC OXENDORF PHOTOGRAPHY STUDIO
1442 N. FRANKLIN PLACE
P.O. BOX 92337
MILWAUKEE, WI 53202
414.273.0654

Iron Block Building
Circa 1861
Milwaukee, WI

Nickel Plating Plant
Allen-Bradley Corporation

Reuss Federal Plaza
Milwaukee, WI

Clients

Wolf + Design

H2D Design

HNTB

Laughlin & Constable

Hoffman York & Compton

Kahler Slater Architects

20th Century Fox

Uihlein Architects

Faison Associates

Historic Preservation

US Dept. of Interior

Publications

Architectural Record

INTERIORS Magazine

US Air Magazine

AIA Journal

ARCHITECTURE

Business Week

Progressive Architecture

Time Magazine

Inland Architect

INC. Magazine

ERIC OXENDORF

E ric Oxendorf has been capturing the spirit of architecture on film for nearly twenty years.

A graduate of the Layton School of Art, he uses a delicate balance of instinct and education to transform rigid architectural structures into poetic statements. The images he creates have won national acclaim for both clients and photographer.

Included in his photographic repertoire are aerials, panoramic/360 degree, interiors, exteriors, and architectural materials.

Eric Oxendorf shoots on location and can travel at a moment's notice. Once on site, he conducts a visual survey to seek out the unique angles and characteristics of a structure's personality.

The result reflects his love of photography and his sensitivity to light and form.

"Space Detail"

Eric Oxendorf

**100 East
Faison Associates**
Milwaukee, WI

Mirage Hotel & Casino
Las Vegas, NV

**Executive Dining Room
Rayovac Corporation**
Madison, WI

**Engineering Library
M.S.O.E.**
Milwaukee, WI

St. Paul's Episcopal Church
Wisconsin

City Hall
Pembroke Pines, FL

City Skyline at Dusk
Milwaukee, WI

ERIC OXENDORF

NCNB Tower
Tampa, FL

Corporate Office Building
Casselberry, FL

Bogk House
Frank Lloyd Wright
Milwaukee, WI
(all images)

Office Park
Orlando, FL
(both images)

PETER AARON

A SENSE OF LIGHT AND SPACE

How did your lighting style evolve? From your study of film?

Yes, that's exactly how it evolved. I studied film in graduate school at NYU, Institute for Color Film and Television and one of my inspirational teachers was a fellow from Czechoslovakia who was a protege of the famous Czech director Milos Forman. His name was Beda Badtke. He taught lighting very very well.

My experience working on movie sets taught me how to light with movie lights such as focusable spots. I learned about flags and other lighting controls that help to light a room. I later found out that film was difficult business to make a living in, and I had a background in photography already, and felt comfortable shooting portraits and landscapes. But now that I had this film lighting knowledge, I started to experiment with interiors. It made perfect sense.

At the time it worked out fabulously well because nobody else was doing it. We were in an age where everyone else was using strobes almost exclusively for lighting interiors. This was about 1973-74. Post Modernism had yet to be discovered and Bauhaus and Modernism were the types of interiors being lighted. This was being done with strobe, because there were large areas of openness, lots of windows and very minimal furnishings. There was no need for pools of light, for low-key movie lighting. So I started doing this unusual method of treating it like a movie set and this new wave of high-tech and Post Modernism came along and the movie lighting was a more appropriate medium for doing pools of light and low key, moody scenes.

So going into interiors was sort of the next logical step at least in terms of still photography?

Absolutely. I liked it because it was like shooting a film, without a crew to worry about. I didn't have to worry about trucks parked on the street, blowing fuses with high amperage cables, damaging people's houses because of heavy equipment and strangers coming in and out. There are fewer people to discuss aesthetics with. Just a magazine editor and an architect. Therefore, I had more creative control. Obviously, films have a lot of creative control. It's just that the budgets are huge and a large number of people are involved. I didn't like that.

Stoller's style seems so perfect for the modernist architecture that was prevalent during his time. Do you feel that your lighting style is as well matched to the Post Modern architecture that has been predominant during much of your career?

Yes. Post Modern really got me going. I could light them as film sets because it is so much like a set design. I rode the wave and now lots of photographers use this method. We'll see where it takes us from here. The deconstructionist work that is now beginning to appear can be handled the same way.

Where do you think it will take us?

What I'm interested in now, and I think what I am pretty sure will happen, is we'll continue to light with hot lights, movie lights, but we'll start to try and use smaller cameras. I happen to like a $2^1/4$ x $3^1/4$ / 6 x 9cm format. We can shoot a bit more off the cuff. We're still in a tungsten mode, but we're using fewer lights so we can do shorter time exposures. We don't have to use lights as much, therefore, we can introduce people. It can become spontaneous again. We can have people, not even posing, but just using a space. We can have a feeling of verité, catching things as they happen. I would like to see smaller format, even 35mm used instead of 4 x 5.

Do you prefer interiors or exteriors?

Actually I prefer doing interiors for the most part, because I feel I have the creative edge. I think that my sense of lighting gets me through a lot of things that are hard for people to do. I think that's where my advantage lies in creative lighting and creative solutions to difficult lighting situations. However, I do love to shoot outdoors, and I like being outdoors and traveling.

Even though you have worked with the movie lighting technique for so many years, has your work evolved? If so, how?

Over the years, much of it has become second nature so that I don't have to think very hard about exposure. In terms of the look, I'm hoping there's a kind of serene feeling to the pictures. A feeling that there's a comfortable composition and that looks natural. I feel

Wisma Dharmala Building
Jakarta, Indonesia
Architect
Paul Rudolph

like it's evolving toward a less formal, more frivolous look. Something that looks, as I said earlier, more spontaneous or off-the-cuff.

I also enjoy taking chances with my work and trying to use fewer lights. Last year I went to the Netherlands to photograph several projects and didn't take any lights with me at all. It made me nervous, but I was able to do the work with available light. I just returned from Japan where I photographed five projects for *Architecture* magazine, and I also left my lights at home.

You want to keep moving in that direction?

Yes. I do. I think my best way to do this is to work more directly with magazines. Then the architects aren't able to dictate the formality that I'm concerned about. So that it's not just a rigid picture of a building where all lines are parallel all of the time, but more atmospheric. That its not necessarily documentary, but has a feeling, a spirit of place. Something which is provocative rather than demonstrative.

You're freer to do that with magazines?

Yes. Magazines are much more interested in that than architects are. Architects don't like *House and Garden* magazine because they feel that their work isn't being well represented. The magazine doesn't care. They want the readers to be pleased, and the readers are more concerned with the human interest and how the architecture interacts with people. Clearly, working for a magazine gives a better chance for experimentation and creativity.

When you are out of town on a job, do you find a local lab to process your film or do you wait and bring it home with you?

It is important for me to see what I'm doing while I'm doing it. One of the reasons is that light sources are different in different interiors. Sometimes I have to test and then it just feels good to know that things are going all right. So I'll go to that lab out of town not just the first day, but often the second and third day. Then I'll bring the last day's undeveloped film home with me and develop it here in New York.

I find that the variation of different labs is small compared to the variation of different light sources. In a studio you would see lab differences easily, but on location you can't see that so easily. Even on exteriors, there are twilight shots, morning shots and mid day shots. Chances are that the lab variations wouldn't show up with all of the strange temperature changes that occur during the day.

I'm not one for holding back film either. I've never had bad experiences with labs ruining film. I've never had bad experiences at airport x-ray machines either. The other thing is that I don't push and pull. I develop all of the film normally and bracket plus 1/2 and minus 1/2 stop so generally I only get two or so really good exposures per view, whereas some other photog-

raphers can maximize that. By pushing and pulling they can get four good exposures of a view. I'm interested in efficiency. I can't spend time after the production examining film and pushing and pulling the balance. I would rather have my one or two perfect exposures and dupe them if necessary rather than waste time going back to the lab.

When architects hire you, why do they ask for you? What is it about your work that they like?

I think the architects want a photograph that can stand on its own as a pretty photograph of their building and at the same time show enough of the building that it represents their work. They like the serenity as I mentioned earlier. They like the possibility of including people. They like it when the best of the lighting is brought out. When I say the best of it, I mean that I don't alter the lighting to make a good photograph in the sense of re-lighting. I augment whatever they've got to make it look really good on film. I think there's a certain guarantee when you hire a photographer with a good reputation that it'll be a less painful experience. That it will occur quicker. That there will be more pictures per day. That there's a better chance that those pictures will be good pictures. I think when you pay a little bit more for someone with a lot of experience, you're getting your money's worth. You're getting more pictures, better pictures, and less fuss.

How many pictures in a day are you talking about?

If it's purely interiors, I usually guarantee about five. Exteriors can skyrocket up to fifteen or even twenty. I like to say to clients that I will produce five interiors in a day. That's the critical thing — interiors. We're talking about lighting, twilight, night shots. I think five is a good amount.

You know that an architectural photographer's hours are horrendous. The day is not limited nine to five by any means. There's a lot of great light early in the morning and fabulous light at twilight. During the middle of the day there are rooms you can shoot that are not near the windows or the outside of the building, so you can always work in there. Some exteriors even look good in the middle of the day. Some spaces cannot be shot with any daylight at all, so you have to work at night. At different times of the year there are long days and other times there are short days. Near December, a day is very short, but fortunately there is much demand for night photography. It doesn't mean that our work is any easier. I would say that this is one of the hardest professions in photography because of the hours. Fashion might be hard, tabletop might be hard, but their hours are a little more confined to normal work day hours. With architecture and interiors many of our jobs are absolute reverse, nocturnal shooting days. It's very hard to recover from a day or two of working all night long.

Do clients go with you on a project? Do the architects go with you?

Architects don't always go with me. I welcome them. I appreciate the help, and I like the walk-through. The walk-through is very important. I like to establish an understanding, a common outlook on how the building should be represented. The architect need not stay the entire time, but I do like to have him or her around for the first part of it. When it's interiors, particularly the ones that require a lot of styling, I don't mind: I encourage the architect to be around for the entire shoot as a gopher, because there is a lot to be solved. There is a tremendous amount of running around. I also, by the same token, tend not to take lunches or dinners off the premises, because the amount of time lost is horrendous. I'd like to see the architect or interior designer go and get the food and bring it back so we can keep working. The only way to get the five or six shots a day is not to leave.

Do you prefer working with architects or interior designers?

Architects. I think in architectural terms. There are many interior designers who are really interior architects, and I like working with them. I don't really like the decorating approach where architecture has fallen by the wayside. Interior designers are often architects, and they often are interior architects. The interior designers for Skidmore, Owings and Merrill are clearly more interested in architecture so to that extent I am interested in working for them. I have worked with many clients in the past who are decorators and I feel a little bit reluctant to work with them because my personal interest is in seeing structure. I want to show rooms, how rooms are put together architecturally. I appreciate the fine points of decorating, but don't really like just showing pillows, couches and chairs. I like to show the room in which they are placed.

Do you try and put people into your work now?

Yes I do. It's a hard thing to do, because you're worried about lighting, exposure, time of day, multiple exposures, but it's important to try to push yourself as far as you can go to get pictures that have a warm and welcoming feeling to them. Sometimes people really bring this to the photograph.

Do you try and place the buildings in their context, or do you prefer to isolate them?

Martinez Hacienda
Taos, New Mexico

93

**San Diego
Convention Center**
San Diego, California
Architects
*Arthur Erickson
Associates; McKinley
Loschky, Marquardt &
Nesholm; Convention
Center Architects*

When you shoot a house or a building, never forget the context. At least consider including it in the picture. A building standing by itself is interesting, but sometimes it's more interesting to show what's next door as well.

In Jakarta I was photographing a big skyscraper which is right on the edge of a sewage canal where a lot of destitute people live in little shacks. I think it made a more interesting picture to show the slums in juxtaposition to the fancy high-rise.

In the particular case of the Jakarta building I'd say that it's not flattering to the building to know that it's right on the edge of the slum, but I was working for the magazine. I think it's fascinating whether it's flattering or not. Therefore, I say do it. If the architect objects, here's a chance to not run the picture. He gets to see the picture often enough before the magazine publishes. I do whatever is best for the photographic image.

What challenges you at the moment? What kind of work would you like to be doing?

I would like to be doing more magazine work where there's some really fascinating subject matter, some new cutting edge architecture, something that may be deconstructive. I want something which requires more of an interpretative approach. Something where the lighting is going to be kind of wild and experimental or there will be people in the shot, or it'll be 35mm. Something new for me.

What is deconstructionist architecture?

Architecture where things look like they're unstable — unstable equilibrium. The real structure of the building is hidden from the eye. It reminds me of a film that was done in the 20s called *The Cabinet of Dr. Calgary* where the set was deconstructionist. There were doors that were trapezoids, ramps instead of walkways, and triangular windows. Everything looked like it was going to fall over. Strange type of thing to do. There's no practical application to deconstructivist architecture. Simply the aesthetics of it. It could never be used for low-cost housing. It's not going to solve any world problems; urban centers, or housing, or shopping malls. It's just a playful thing.

It's even more playful than Post Modern?

Yes. It's like stage sets. It's something fun to shoot but

I wouldn't want to live there. Let's face it, Post Modernism is much better for photography than it is for actual living. There's something about Post Modernism that has no longevity. It's playing with the designs and artifacts of buildings from the last century or the last millennium. There's no solidity to them. They're not meant to last for the ages. They're great for photography though.

Do you treat different styles of architecture differently when you photograph them or light them? Are you conscious of treating them different?

I treat them somewhat differently. Often with Modernist style I will just want blanket lighting. Since it is so minimal looking, usually big, broad, soft lights are more appropriate than these pinpoint spots whereas with Post Modernism you might just want to put a pinpoint of light here and a pinpoint of light there and have it be very low key and spotty. I think I have a lighting style that is somewhat recognizable and more to the point, the lighting is dictated by the space, by the architect and the lighting designer. My ideal lighting is to look as though I didn't light it at all; as if the lighting was designed by the lighting designer. My job is to fill it in, spike it up, bring it to the epitome of what it was meant to do in the first place, before I got there.

How long did you work directly with Ezra Stoller?

I worked with Ezra for about two years. I assisted him on maybe thirty jobs in all. It was spotty. I wanted to do my own work. I learned a lot from him, but I never was really there on a day-to-day basis. I was always freelancing and often hard to get. I found that I wanted to work for myself, and I wanted to learn as much from Ezra as I could. I'm not sure I was such a great assistant, because I was so anxious to do my own work.

What did you learn from him?

Ezra taught me plenty of tricks. He taught business practices so I knew how to approach clients. I knew what to do about fee structures, availability, and all kinds of attitudes toward speaking with the clients and spending time with them. I learned all kinds of things about technique. What film stock to use — whether or not to push. How to deal in black and white. Was black and white important? Should I shoot all jobs in black and white and color? What about styling? What about storing negatives? How many sheets should I shoot for each view? What should I show the client? Should I show them everything I shoot, every view

Lobby – Dance Theatre of the Netherlands
Rotterdam, Netherlands
Architect
Office of Metropolitan Architecture, Rem Koolhaas

Renovation – The New York Public Library
Fifth Avenue, New York
Architects
Carrere and Hastings
Reconstruction Architects
Davis Brody & Associates

that I shoot? Lots of stuff like that. Tricks about lighting. Particularly tricks about exposing. Tricks about what camera to use, filters, lots of stuff like that and then I took off from there. Some things I disagreed with, other things I augmented.

What did you learn esthetically?

Ezra has a very strong eye. He makes big statements with his camera so I learned that it's OK to be interpretative. I learned an attitude that he had which is that we are not artists, we're craftsmen. We're hired to show somebody else's art. If we get too caught up in ourselves, we might fall down on the job so Ezra taught me that if I'm going to be jazzy with my camera, I ought to at least respect the architect's work since he's the primary artist. So I learned how to walk that fine line of being a craftsman/artist, revealing the work of another artist.

Is that still how you work? How you see things? Is it still your idea of what your task is?

Yes. I still consider myself to be a craftsman rather than an artist and that my job is to show the subject matter in the best possible light. I'm not trying to

make it look less than it could be, but more. I think that I do take more liberties than Ezra ever did. That is, I will distort the original if it makes a better picture. I think I do use wider angle lenses than Ezra was comfortable with, and I know that I shoot more Polaroids than he ever dreamed he would. Polaroids have helped me to refine lighting more than he needed to. The wide-angle lenses have created more distortion but also more drama, so I've taken more liberties with the original than he ever did. Of course, I think he's a fabulous photographer and that he's gotten some of the greatest images of architecture I've seen anywhere.

Do you go out and shoot for yourself? Do you have any personal projects you're working on?

I've started some personal projects. I need to do more of them. One has been the work on the New York subway stations that fascinate me. How old they are, how rickety they look and how much hidden beauty there is lurking from the old days. I also have a house in the Hudson River Valley, and I particularly like photographing the land there. That's something I do little by little, but I would like to pick up the pace on that.

What would you say to someone starting out who

finds themselves photographing a lot of mundane buildings?

That's simple. The personal projects are very important for him or her, because you're not going to get the assignments at first. You've got to go to the Fifth Avenue Library yourself, or to Union Station in St. Louis, or to the Palace of Fine Arts in San Francisco. There's no way you're going to get the good assignments unless you show people that you can do it. So, hopefully you're compelled to do it. You can make a good portfolio that way.

What would you say to them when they're on the job photographing a strip shopping center?

A great way to experiment and test is to treat mundane assignments as tests. When I'm shooting something very dull like a shopping center, I make sure that I do something new. I'll find out about filters or find out about smaller format, graduated neutral density filters, shutter speeds visa vis people moving around in the shot. Anything I can do to take away the boring, dull aspects of the assignment.

Do you prefer using tungsten or daylight films?

I almost always use the tungsten films. They handle the longer exposure better and have a softer contrast range which is usually helpful. If I am shooting under daylight conditions I will add an 85B filter.

You told me last year that you sold all of your strobe equipment. Do you regret doing so and would you like to have it back?

No, not really. There are times when I could use strobe, but I am trying to lighten my load and having the strobes would mean more cases to bring with me. I've found that I can work with tungsten and available light to do almost anything.

What equipment do you use?

I have an old Sinar Standard 4 x 5. I also have a good set of lenses (47, 65, 75, 90, 121, 150, 210 and 300) and two roll film backs I use when there are people in the scene or the lighting conditions are changing rapidly.

Reprinted with permission from **View Camera** *magazine.*

Esto Photographics
222 Valley Place
Mamaroneck, NY 10543
914.698.4060
Fax: 914.698.1033

Architects
Kohn Pederson Fox Associates

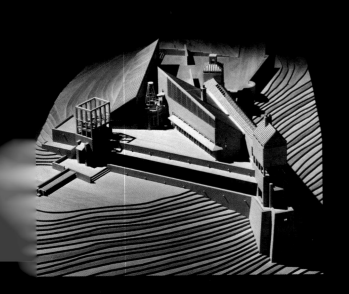

JOCK POTTLE

J ock Pottle photographs architectural models. After a number of years as a location photographer, he is now concentrating on the documentation of models in his well-equipped studio. Pottle controls light to make a model come alive without losing sight of the faith and the humor involved in translating a scale model into a full-sized building.

Jock Pottle is represented by Esto which helps arrange his assignments and maintains a valuable photo library for architects and publishers.

Architect
Harry Elson

JOCK POTTLE

Architects
Kohn Pederson Fox Associates

Architects
Richard Meier & Partners

Jock Pottle

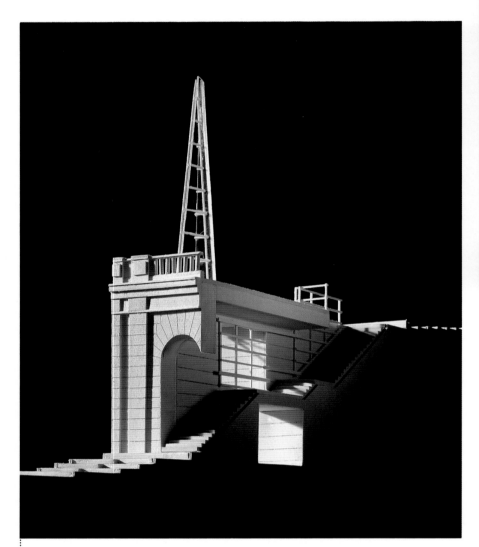

Architects
Skidmore, Owings and Merrill

Architects
Weiss Manfredi

Architect
Karen Van Lengen

Architects
Richard Meier & Partners

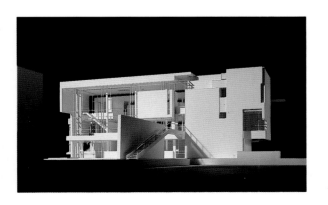

Jock Pottle

Architects
Pei Cobb Freed

Architects
Kohn Pederson Fox Associates

Architects
*James Stewart Polshek
and Partners*

Architects
Gwathmey Siegel Associates

Architects
Hanrahan Meyers

PETER RENERTS STUDIO
2210 SUPERIOR VIADUCT
CLEVELAND, OH 44113
216.781.2440

Private Gardens
Virginia
Landscape Architect
Russell Page

Mansion Renovation
Bratenahl, OH
Designers
The Oliver Design Group

Clients

The Arris Group

Copeland, Novak,
Israel Architects

Don M. Hisaka
Architects

Richard Fleischman
Architects

Forest City
Development

The Jerde Partnership

Keeva J. Kekst
Architects

Melvin Simon &
Assoc. Developers

The Oliver Design
Group

RTKL Architects

Wyant & Associates
Designers

Guest House and Grounds
Virginia
Landscape Architect
Russell Page

Publications

Interior Design
Magazine

Architectural Digest

Progressive
Architecture

Horticulture Magazine

Building Design
& Construction

World Space Design

Kukan (Japan)

PETER RENERTS

Peter Renerts was drawn to architecture in his university days at CWRU through a friendship with a foreign architecture student. "We played a lot of chess, spoke in French, and debated the meaning of Bauhaus.", he recalls. The debate goes on, but now Peter takes fine photographs to bolster his side.

Peter's style is direct, based on the principles of "clarity with drama" … "look for volume and geometry that quickly, forcefully reveals a space or structure, and does so with beauty." Strong compositions result from his creative control over visual elements. Through 16 years of shooting architecture he has refined his lighting techniques to achieve the captivating subtleties that are his hallmark.

Laura Travis is Peter's talented Senior Photographer; she brings additional depth of vision and a fine styling sense to all of their projects. Peter's clients appreciate his thorough preparations for each job: homework that allows concentration not on problems but rather, on creativity. "Our goal is to create effective and appealing images that have the maximum marketing value for our clients."

Grand Rotunda, The Fashion Mall
Plantation, FL
Developer
Melvin Simon & Associates
Technical
Keeva J. Kekst Architects

PETER RENERTS

Cafe Paradiso
Cleveland, OH
Architecture/Design
The Oliver Design Group

Private Residence
Northeast Ohio
Architect
Wilson Architectural Group
Project Architect
Jack Hawk
Interior Design
Mark Wyant & Associates

The Society Center
Cleveland, OH
Architects
Cesar Pelli Architects

(Building to right)
BP America Building
Cleveland, OH
Architects
*Hellmuth, Obata &
Kassabaum Associates*

PETER RENERTS

Private Residence
Northeast Ohio
Architect
Wilson Architectural Group
Project Architect
Jack Hawk
Interior Design
Mark Wyant & Assoc.

Signature Square
Ofc Building
Beachwood, OH
Design Architects
Don M. Hisaka Architects
Technical
Keeva J. Kekst Architects

Entertainment Level, The Mall of America
Bloomington, MN
Design Architects
The Jerde Partnership
Consortium
HGA/KKE Architects Minneapolis

109

CERVIN ROBINSON
251 WEST 92ND STREET, #10E
NEW YORK, NY 10025
212.873.0464

CERVIN ROBINSON

Work has appeared in, among others, the following publications:

A & U

Architectural Digest

Architectural Design

Architectural Record

Architectural Forum

Architecture PLUS

Art in America

Artforum

Bauwelt

H & G

The New York Times Magazine

The Architectural Review

Designers whose buildings Robinson has photographed:

Edward Larrabee Barnes

Peter Eisenman

Ellerbe Becket

Roger Ferri

Michael Graves

Hardy Holzman Pfeiffer

Philip Johnson

R.M. Kliment & Frances Halsband

Kohn Pedersen Fox

Mies van der Rohe

Charles Moore

Pei Cobb Freed

Cesar Pelli

Kevin Roche

Paul Rudolph

Eero Saarinen

Venturi, Scott Brown

Heron Building
New York City

House
Vermont
Turner Brooks

House
Long Island, New York
**Diane Love,
Mark Matthews**

Little House Room
Metropolitan Museum
Frank Lloyd Wright

House
Woodstock, New York
R.M. Kliment & Frances Halsband

CERVIN ROBINSON

Computer Building
Princeton University, New Jersey
R.M. Kliment & Frances Halsband

Currier Gallery
Manchester, NH
Hardy Holzman Pfeiffer

STEVE ROSENTHAL
59 MAPLE STREET
AUBURNDALE, MA 02166
617.244.2986
FAX: 617.244.9824

Hood Museum, Dartmouth College
Hanover, NH
Architects
Charles Moore with Chad Floyd of Centerbrook, 1985

Steve Rosenthal

Clients

Edward Larrabee Barnes

The Beacon Companies

Boston Properties

Cambridge Seven Associates

Centerbrook/Charles Moore

Gwathmey/Siegel

Graham Gund Architects

Kallmann McKinnell & Wood

Herbert Newman & Partners

Notter Finegold & Alexander

Pei Cobb Freed & Partners

Moshe Safdie & Associates

Skidmore Owings & Merrill

The Architects Collaborative

Benjamin Thompson & Associates

Museum of Fine Arts, West Wing Addition
Boston, MA
Architects
I.M. Pei & Partners (I.M. Pei, Design Partner) 1981

Hynes Auditorium
Boston, MA
Architects
Kallmann, McKinnell and Wood, 1988

75 State Street
Boston, MA
Architects
Graham Gund Architects and Skidmore
Owings and Merrill (Chicago Office)
Developer
The Beacon Companies, 1989

SCOTT SANDERS, PHOTOGRAPHER
9638 SUTTON GREEN COURT
VIENNA, VA 22181
703.281.2538
FAX: 703.281.1071

The Robert Trent Jones Golf Club is very private yet very inviting.
The Challenge: To capture the design and elegance of a project that fulfills the requirements of architect, designer, and contractor.

Architects/Designers

James Langenheim/ Pasadena

Chapman, Coyle, Chapman, Atlanta

H. Chambers & Assoc

Architectural Interiors

Chapel Valley Landscapes

Harry Weese Associates

Alex Chapman/ Toronto

W.G. Reed Architects

Interior Architects

LaPierre Associates

Nygaard Design/ Toronto

Omni Construction

Deupi Associates

Wamack, Humphries/ Dallas

Wisnewski-Blair

Davis & Carter

Corporations/ Hotels

American Express/ New York

Lowes L'enfant Plaza Hotel

Casa Marina Resort/ Key West

Prudential Properties

Marriott Corporation

Ramada Renissance

U.S. Steel

Snyder-Hunt

Mobil

Washington Hilton

Capital Hilton

Club Med

Publications

Metropolitan Home

Commercial Renovation

Regardies

Washington Home & Garden

Washington Post Magazine

Country Home Magazine

Scott Sanders

"I wish you could be here with me right now and see this"

Our desire to share beauty with someone else is a strong one. Scott Sanders approaches each assignment with this thought in mind: that these are those beautiful places whose dramatic moments must be shared.

In the business of golf club and resort photography, those thoughts must be succinctly crystallized for the client. Whether on assignment for Club-Med or for the Marriott Corporation the results must be the same: share the moment.

Scott Sanders specializes in photographing resorts, golf courses and private clubs. Combining the skills of landscape design, as well as architectural and interior design photography, Scott brings with him a commitment to capture beauty, art and a complete sense of the project.

Many of his clients are architects and designers who submit their work for competition. However, that same body of work must also serve the needs of the builder or the marketing division. With that in mind, Scott Sanders looks for the common thread that will successfully and artfully tie the assignment together.

The Clubhouse at Robert Trent Jones Golf Club
Lake Manassas, VA
Chapman, Coyle, Chapman, Atlanta
Omni Construction
Washington, D.C.

The Beautiful and dangerous 11th hole
Part of a magazine photo essay on great par 3 holes of the Mid-Atlantic
Designer
Robert Trent Jones

SCOTT SANDERS

Trophy Room at The Dominion Country Club

Dining Room at The Dominion Country Club
Serving as centerpiece of the club.

Island hole 4th
Swan Point, MD
Part of a U.S. Steel property development. Swan Point Marketing and a USX Annual Report.

"The Dominion Club"
A Snyder Hunt Development in Richmond, VA
Architects
Chapman, Coyle, Chapman, Atlanta

124

Suites at Private Club
Washington, DC
Interior Design
Alex Chapman. Toronto

SHIELDS-MARLEY PHOTOGRAPHY
117 SOUTH VICTORY STREET
LITTLE ROCK, AR 72201
501.372.6148
FAX: 501.371.9517

**Perry County Courthouse Restoration
and New Construction**
New Augusta, MS
Architect: Albert & Lewis Architects
Hattiesburg, MS
*1993 Outstanding Renovation Award,
Mississippi Historical Society*

Clients

Albert & Lewis
Architects

Amanda Adcock
Interiors/ASID

William Henry Asti
Architects

Baldwin & Shell
Construction Co.

Phyllis T. Billingsley,
ASID

Mary Lee Blocker, ASID

Brackett-Krennerich
Architects

Brooks Jackson & Don
Johnson Architects

Burt Taggart &
Associates Architects

Connelly Abbott Dunn
Architects

Cooper Communities,
Inc.

Cornerstone Architects

Design Alliance/
K.C. Poole, ASID

The Design Exchange

Garver & Garver
Engineers

Godfrey, Bassett,
Kuykendall &
Campbell Architects

Quest House Inns, Inc.

Thomas Harding
Construction Co.

Hensel Phelps
Construction Co.

Interior Insight Inc.

John D. Jarrard
Architects

Marshall Clements
Interiors

Mott Mobley
McGowan & Griffin
Architects

Nabholz Construction
Corporation

A.W. Nelson Architects

John Sanders Architects

The Stuck Associates
Architects

United States Air Force

Witsell Evans Rasco
Architects

Wittenberg Delony &
Davidson Architects

DeAnn Shields-Marley

The nature of Ms. Shields-Marley's art work reflects a strong graphic design philosophy, which ultimately began with a background in fine art photography. After attending advanced training courses at such renowned schools as R.I.T. College of Graphic Arts and Photography, Maine Photographic Workshops, Winona International School of Professional Photography and Anderson Ranch Arts Center, she began to integrate technique with her visual acuity to capture the art of architecture. Her extraordinary talent was quickly recognized as her photography won awards for clients and was printed in such national publications as *Kitchen and Bath Concepts* and the *Architectural Record*. About her photography of Arkansas's largest coliseum the architect George Wittenburg wrote, *"DeAnn's ability to record accurately and artistically the relationships of such intrinsic design factors as form, light and color helped us capture the whole forest — no small feat considering the size and scope of this large multi-use facility."* Brooks Jackson also writes, *"DeAnn is a professional and an excellent photographer. I give her credit for the success of our company brochure, as well as winning design awards."*

Toronto City Hall Complex
Toronto, Canada

Downtown Toronto
Toronto, Canada

DeAnn Shields-Marley

Hill Road House
Renovation of 1922 sunporch
Interior Designers
Chandler & Associates

Overlook Drive House
Little Rock, AR
Interior Designers
Interior Insight

DeAnn Shields-Marley

Maloof Barn
Anderson Ranch Arts Center
Aspen, CO
Restoration Architect
Harry Teague

Fischer Photography Center
Anderson Ranch Arts Center
Aspen, CO
Architect
Harry Teague

Hemingway House
Little Rock, AR
Restoration Architect
Witsell Evans Rasco Architects

NICK SPRINGETT PHOTOGRAPHY
1316 MAPLE STREET
SANTA MONICA, CA 90405
310.271.7514

Kevin Farrell Design Associates

Clients

William D. Fauber AIA

Steven Ball & Associates AIA

Ernest Grunsteld AIA

Projects Architecture

Clive Wilson Interior Design

Interni Design

L.A. Design

Southby's International Realty

Kaufman Broad

Beverly Hills Hotel

J.M.B. Properties

McCann Erickson Advertising

Publications

Home Magazine

Condé Nast Traveler

Estates Internationale

S.C. Home & Garden

Interiors Magazine

Designers West

Luis Ortega Design

William D. Fauber A.I.A.

130

NICK SPRINGETT

I f one were to define Nick Springett's photography, they would describe his extraordinary balance of composition and his exquisite sense of lighting. These carefully detailed and executed elements produce a finished product that is at once classical and natural.

Nick's talent has captured great architecture, interior design, major developments, landscapes and works of sculpture, painting and abstract art. Working closely with his clients, Nick is sensitive to their needs and works from the best perspective for the subject; from close up studio shots though a spectrum, all the way to mountain tops and aerials.

His client list is a veritable who's who in architecture, interior design, real estate development, advertising and art. His work has been internationally published and used as a major tool by grateful clients for magazines, annual reports, exhibitions, catalogs and brochures. Nick is based in Los Angeles and has worked there for the past ten years. His client affiliations often take him to different locales and he delights in utilizing his expertise and careful attention to detail for each new challenge.

Marriott/Century City

Century Plaza Towers

St. James' Club/L.A.

BOB SWANSON
SWANSON IMAGES
259 CLARA STREET
SAN FRANCISCO, CA 94107
415.495.6507
FAX: 415.495.6531

The Daisy Hotel,
Lobby Stairs

"The Dry"
Shower Area

"The Dry"
Window to Offices

The "Building
Inspector's House
from the Daisy Hotel
Personal Work
(All work on this
page is from the
forthcoming book,
"Home Sweet Jerome")

Clients

Fee Munson Ebert

Gensler and Assoc.

Daniel, Mann,
Johnson, &
Mendenhall

Ehrlich Rominger

Backen Arrigoni
& Ross

Famous Design
Architects

Susan Hedin,
Interior Sources

AT&T

Plant Construction
Company

Rudolph & Sletten

Apersey Construction

Publications

Architectural Record

Interiors

Designers West

Visual Merchandising
& Store Design

Northern California
Home & Garden

Phoenix Home &
Garden

Lighting Design &
Application

BOB SWANSON

Bob Swanson's photographs are created with the goals of the architect and designer firmly in mind. His aim is to capture the complex dimensions of style, grace and creativity, while stunning the viewer into recognition of the individual designer's aesthetic intentions. His passion and commitment to technical fluency springs from his desire to capture a building's inner vitality, a perspective which finds its roots in twenty years of experience as a builder and designer. This involvement in the architectural industry adds an important dimension to Bob Swanson's unique vision and dedication.

"I know the type of sweat involved in achieving architectural greatness, and the complex collaborations needed to turn plans into finished structures. I consider my passion for photography as an intrinsic part of that collaboration." For these reasons, Bob Swanson's photographs have been widely reproduced for magazine articles, client ads, brochures, annual reports and other marketing materials.

The Temple Emanu-El

BOB SWANSON

**Port of Oakland,
Executive Reception Area**
Commercial Work

**Genstar Container,
Conference Room**
Commercial Work

**Delancey Street
Foundation
Headquarters,
Inner Courtyard**
Commercial Work

**Historic San Francisco
Club's Natatorium**
Commercial Work

**Sylvester Mansion,
Foyer and Living Room**
Residential Work

**Ornstein/Schatz
Residence, Backyard**
Residential Work

**Rodin's "The Kiss"
at "La Petite Trianon"**
Residential Work

Powder Box Church, Entry
Residential Work

BRIAN VANDEN BRINK
P.O. Box 419
ROCKPORT, ME 04856
207.236.4035

Private Residence
Camden, ME
Architect
Christian Fasoldt
Photographed for
Down East Magazine

Clients

Cabot Stains

L.L. Bean

Center for Creative
Imaging

Vermont Castings

Thomas Moser,
Cabinetmakers

World Book
Encyclopedia

Kodak

Stewart Tabori & Chang

Houghton Mifflin

Sasaki Associates,
Architects

The Architects
Collaborative

Ricci Associates,
Architects

Perry Dean Rogers &
Partners

Cannon Architects

Winton Scott, Architect

Symmes Maini McKee,
Architects

Stephen Blatt Architects

VanDam & Renner,
Architects

Harriman Associates

Orcutt-Simons,
Architects

Aroostook County, ME

Publications

Architecture

Architectural Digest

Architectural Record

Atlantic Magazine

Decorating Remodeling

Elle Decor

Historic Preservation

Home

House Beautiful

House & Garden

Inland Architect

Smithsonian Books

Art New England

Down East

Boston Globe Magazine

Washington Post
Magazine

Making maximum use of natural light in photographing architecture has been Brian Vanden Brink's trademark for the last fifteen years. Recognizing the select moment and being in the right place at the right time produces photographs that go beyond mere documentation to a more personal portrait of architecture in its environment. Patience, vision and an awareness of the beauty of nature's light are the tools that Brian uses to produce evocative photographs of architecture on a more human and approachable scale.

Ruggles House, Built 1818
Columbia Falls, ME

**Sweetwood Continuing
Care Community**
Williamstown, MA
Architects
The Architects Collaborative

**Portland Head
Light Museum**
Portland, ME
Architects
*VanDam & Renner
Restoration Architects/
Woodworth Assoc.*

Willa Cather House
Red Cloud, NE
Photographed for
Smithsonian Books

Shaker Interior
Sabbath Day Lake, ME

BRIAN VANDEN BRINK

Private Residence
West Rockport, ME
Architect
Stephen G. Smith

Fort Knox, Built 1840
Bucksport, ME

Private Residence
Washington, CT
Designer
Robert Currie
Photographed for
House & Garden

CERVIN ROBINSON

THE TASK OF AN ARCHITECTURAL PHOTOGRAPHER

We architectural photographers like to think you can tell our pictures apart, that the work of each of us speaks with an individual voice. This individuality, when it has existed, has always come (1) from the perspectives from which we approached our subjects — head-on and objective, for instance, or oblique and experimental; (2) from what we chose to include in a picture; and (3) from our craftsmanship (or lack of it). To judge by what appears currently in architectural magazines, there is less individuality in our work now than there used to be. I think there are two linked reasons for the change. One is that the use of color transparency film has shifted our priorities away from how we approach a subject and what we include in a picture, to craftsmanship alone; the other reason is that a turn away from individuality seems a prudent one when we are working directly for architects — and it is architects, not magazines, that are now paying our bills.

Reversal transparency films, "chromes," from which color reproductions in magazines are made, make special technical demands of us. Exposures must be more precise than for negative film, so we bracket them. Because interiors are more seductive in color than they are in black and white, we take more of them; and then we devote much of our attention to reconciling incompatible sources of light (fluorescent with daylight or tungsten illumination), to reducing excessive contrast, or to improving the purity of illumination. After we have spent hours gelling lights or have had an assistant run up and down flights of stairs to manipulate light switches while we make a set of time exposures on each of a series of sheets of film; have painted with light the seats of a whole theater; or have merely adjusted flash heads and umbrellas between tests with Polaroid film to achieve some plausible result without including in a picture either light stand legs or the reflection of an umbrella from some polished surface — after we have gone to this much trouble, sad to say, we have a vested interest in thinking the often humdrum result remarkable.

But to present such machinations as our most significant skills is like claiming that our primary skills as photographers in black and white lie in dodging and burning. Unfortunately, it is where we put our efforts that we get special returns, and the pictures in architectural magazines suggest that our work is controlled and craftsmanly but pictorially ordinary and largely indistinguishable as the work of individual photographers.

If this overemphasis on only one part of picture making is almost inevitable when we make chromes, it has been reinforced by the economics of magazine publishing. When color photographs became the norm in architectural magazines, the costs of reproduction and of commissioned photography turned out to be such that magazines began asking the architects whose buildings were to be published to foot the bills from photographers. At that point we found that, though the purpose of our pictures might be magazine publication, we were no longer working for editors but for architects alone. And though these are people who could hardly imagine not asserting their creative individuality at a client's expense, we become prudently low profile in exercising our own individuality. When an architect nudges us to take particular pictures, they are ones that show a building as he hoped it would look. By contrast, an editor's nudges used to encourage us to accomplish two other things that may actually be mutually irreconcilable: (1) to show a building as he thought it actually looked and (2) to do so in the form of the exciting pictures that would draw readers to his magazine. Exciting pictures tend to be idiosyncratic. Back in the 1950s and 1960s, photographer, editor, and architect could share a common faith in modernism, yet each had separate and sometimes healthily conflicting goals. A photographer, like an editor, could achieve a degree of journalistic integrity and an individual voice. Now, our knowledge of the side on which our bread is buttered sends us into frenzies of technical industriousness that are designed to please but not to upstage our client architects. We were, to a degree, expressive individuals; we are now so many anonymous renderers.

For the architect at least it may look as though there are clear advantages to the new arrangement. Under the older system it often seemed to him that editors were too easily satisfied with the photographs they commissioned. It is true that an architect may well be able to budget more time and money to the taking of his own buildings than an editor could spend. But the latter may also be able to make a more objective judgement of a building's individual qualities and relative significance. In the end, all three — architect, editor, and photographer — are losers in that a duller and safer, journalism makes architecture itself the duller and more parochial.

Always, insurmountably good reasons present themselves for the things we do that make our pictures duller. A lack of people in architectural photographs? When multiple exposures don't make their inclusion quite possible, bracketing makes it unlikely that the best-exposed chrome will have the best arrangement of people. Exclusive use of color pictures even at a time when architects are looking again at black and white? A single impression of black ink offset onto the cheaper paper that suffices for color reproduction is so drab as not to be worth making. Probably editors think they are giving architects all they want, while architects think magazines are giving them all they can.

Photographers, meanwhile, are only hired guns.

Architectural magazines used to offer their readers (and their photographers) an alternative to the exemplary new buildings that now fill them, one that allowed a photographer even more opportunity than usual to speak with an individual voice. That subject was the real world of older or ordinary buildings into which the new were designed to be built and that make up the cities and other communities in which most of us actually live and work. True, in the 1950s and 1960s it was easier to show these subjects as alternatives: new buildings in magazines were Modern (seductively photographed), whereas the older world was pre-Modern (photographed objectively or even critically). Then, magazines were enriched by the combination. Now, I suspect, editors think that anything comparable is impossible if only because a newly-published building now, likely as not, itself speaks in a historical or vernacular tongue.

But we have now passed from the 1980s, when blindness to the real world was in character, to the 1990s, when all the bills have come due. The roles of black-and-white and color photographs have become reversed: black-and-white pictures, once drably routine, though versatile, are now special; seductive color pictures have become boringly routine. I want to suggest that some enterprising architectural magazine editor take a hint from the world of advertising, where duotone black-and-white reproductions stand out as exciting and almost dangerous in a sea of routinely seductive color, and talk more adventurous architects into having us photograph selected new buildings for publication in black and white. I also want to suggest that he or she commission us to show, in black and white, the strengths and weaknesses of the real world out there that architectural magazines have for a generation neglected. Both architecture and the communities in which buildings are erected will benefit — and the pictures we take can once again show themselves to be the work of individual photographers.

PETER VANDERWARKER, PHOTOGRAPHER
28 PRINCE STREET
WEST NEWTON, MA 02165
617.964.2728

Dicara Law Offices
Boston, MA
Architects
Jung/Brannen Associates

Trinity Church / John Hancock Tower
Boston, MA
Architects
H.H. Richardson / Harry Cobb,
I.M. Pei and Partners
Aspen Design Conference

PETER VANDERWARKER

Peter Vanderwarker is a graduate of Phillips Academy, Andover and has a Bachelor of Architecture degree from the University of California, Berkeley.

Peter is the author and photographer of *Boston, Then and Now*, published in 1982, and his current book, *Cityscapes of Boston* is co-authored with Boston Globe architectural critic Robert Campbell and published by Houghton Mifflin.

In 1989 Mr. Vanderwarker received a grant from the National Endowment for the Arts to document Boston's Central Artery Project. In 1992 he received Institute Honors from the American Institute of Architects.

Albany State Capital Interior
Albany, NY
Architect
Samuel Fuller

PETER VANDERWARKER

Post Office Square Park
Boston, MA
Architects
*Ellenzweig Associates and
The Halvorson Company*

Naisbitt Condominium,
Cambridge, MA
Cary Tamarkin/Tim Techler Design, Boston
Boston Globe Magazine

Team Disney Building
Orlando, FL
Architect
Arata Isozaki

Hynes Memorial Convention Center
Boston, MA
Architect
Kallmann, McKinnell, and Wood,
Progressive Architecture

Schwab House
Woodstock, VT
Architect
Ertel Associates Architecture
Woodstock

222 Berkley Street
Boston, MA
Architects
Robert A.M. Stern

Lloyd's of London
Headquarters Exterior
London, England
Architecture
Richard Rogers Partnership

Lloyd's of London Headquarters Exterior
London, England
Architecture
Richard Rogers Partnership

Coastal Cement
Boston, MA
Architects
HMFH Architects,
Cambridge, MA
Progressive Architecture

Furman University Art Studio
Greenville, SC
Architects
Perry, Dean, Rogers,
Boston, MA
Architectural Record

**Hynes Memorial
Convention Center**
Boston, MA
Architect
*Kallman, McKinnell,
and Wood*
Progressive Architecture

Becton Dickinson Headquarters Interior
Fair Lawn, NJ
Architect
Kallmann, McKinnell, and Wood
Progressive Architecture

Rowes Wharf Exterior
Boston, MA
Architects
Skidmore, Owings, and Merrill
Chicago Architectural Record

MATT WARGO
4236 MAIN STREET
PHILADELPHIA, PA 19127
215.483.1211
FAX: 215.483.9350

The Benjamin Franklin Dining Room
U.S. Department of State
Washington, DC
Architects
John Blatteau Associates

S.A.B.H. U.S., Inc.
Philadelphia, PA
Architects
Floss Barber, Inc.

Private Residence
Ocean City, NJ
Serge Robin Interior Design
Feltoon Parry Associates, Inc.

Clients

Charles E. Broudy
& Associates
Philadelphia, PA

Buttrick White
& Burtis Architects
New York

Daniel V. Scully
Architects
Peterborough, NH

Floss Barber, Inc.
Philadelphia, PA

Grad Associates
Newark, NJ

The Hillier Group
Princeton, NJ

International Design
Group
Toronto, Canada

KPA Design Group
Philadelphia, PA

Payette Associates
Boston, MA

RTKL Associates
Ft. Lauderdale, FL

Vitetta Group
Philadelphia, PA

Venturi, Scott Brown
Associates
Philadelphia, PA

Zeidler Roberts
Partnership
Toronto, Canada

Publications

Architectural Digest

Architecture

Architectural Record

Interior Design

Interior Magazine

Progressive
Architecture

Matt Wargo Photography has specialized for 10 years in architectural and interiors photography for architects, retailers, developers, and corporations, as well as interior and graphic designers. Assignments from across the U.S. and worldwide have ranged from commissions for individual rooms to entire museums and new hotels. The images are direct but evocative, balancing technical expertise with sensitivity to design intentions.

With over 300 projects since 1982, the work is characterized by personal attention to the quality of the shoot, from planning through printing and publication. A dedication to clear, consistent communication with clients assures a high degree of aesthetic and technical collaboration, which is reflected in the long-standing associations with clients. Projects photographed have been featured in American, European and Japanese publications, winning widespread exposure for clients. A full studio, a comprehensive printing service, and a complete archival system facilitates accurate and responsive service to clients, publications, public relations and advertising organizations.

National Gallery
London, England
Architects
Venturi, Scott Brown & Associates

MATT WARGO

Boyd's
Philadelphia, PA
Architects
Charles E. Broudy & Associates

OLC
Philadelphia, PA
Architects
Wesley Wei Architects

U.S. Healthcare
Blue Bell, PA
Architects
The Hillier Group

MATT WARGO

Team Disney Building
Orlando, FL
Architects
Arata Isozaki & Associates

Caesar's Palace
Las Vegas, NV

McDonald Medical Research Laboratories
Los Angeles, CA
Architects
Venturi, Scott Brown & Associates

157

DAVID WHITTAKER PHOTOGRAPHER, INC.
276 CARLAW AVENUE, SUITE #307
TORONTO, ONT., CANADA M4M-3L1
1.416.466.0558
FAX: 1.416.466.0989

Skydome Theatre
Designer: Marshall
Cummings & Associates

Club Pro
Designer: II by IV

Dun & Bradstreet Software
Designer: Corplan

Clients
Interior Designers

Marshall Cummings
& Assoc.

Cecconi Simone

Yabu Pushelberg

Raymond Chiapetta &
Assoc.

Inger Barlett & Assoc.

Mole White & Assoc.

Donald Bell
Consultants

Bullock & Assoc.

Atkinson McLeod

Allsteel

Publications

Interior Design
Magazine

Interiors Magazine

Contract Magazine

Financial Post
Magazine

Nikkei Architecture
Magazine

Progressive
Architecture Magazine

**Goodman and Goodman
Law Offices**
Designer: Marshall
Cummings & Associates

Club Pro
Designer: II by IV

DAVID WHITTAKER

David Whittaker began his professional career in photography as a still photographer for feature films. By studying and working with several academy award winning Directors of Photography, he came to appreciate the difficult task of simple lighting and the art of setting moods within a photograph.

"Lighting and camera angles must lead a viewer through the photograph, and in so doing will inevitably enhance the viewer's perception of the space that is being photographed."

David Whittaker has earned awards for his corporate work from The American Centre for Design, as well as in numerous competitions of communication arts, graphics, and applied arts. His client list consists of many well renowned interior designers from the United States and Canada.

DAVID WHITTAKER

DAVID WHITTAKER

Axis Showroom
Designer:
Cecconi Eppstadt Simone

**(Inset) Sunrise
Department Store**
Taiwan
Designer
Yabu Pushelberg

Signor Angelo Store
Designer:
Yabu Pushelberg

Ocean's Restaurant
Designer:
Yabu Pushelberg

KENNETH M. WYNER PHOTOGRAPHY
7012 WESTMORELAND AVENUE
TAKOMA PARK, MD 20912
301.495.9475

Kaiser Permanente
McLean, VA
Architect
HDR

OSEH Shalom
Laurel, MD
Architect: Travis Price
Takoma Park, MD

Clients
HDR Architects
HOK Architects
Ellerbe Becket
Architects
CRSS Architects
Columbia Design
Collective Architects
SOM Architects
Jersey Devil Architects
H. Chambers Co.
Price & Partners
SH & G Architects

Publications
Architecture
Architectural Lighting
Architecture &
Urbanism
Interior Design
Landscape
Architecture
Regardies
Restaurant & Hotel
Design
Progressive
Architecture
Popular Science
Garden Design
Architectural Record

KENNETH M. WYNER

Ken Wyner has been taking photographs for over twenty years: From experience as a fine arts photographer in the Washington, D.C. area, to extensive travel in Iran and Afghanistan, capturing portraits of the land and people. His work has been exhibited at the Corcoran Gallery of Art, and the Museum of Modern Art in Washington.

Mr. Wyner specialized in fashion photography for a number of years, before moving exclusively into corporate and architectural work, which he has now been doing for over a decade. As Mr Wyner states, "What has always drawn me to photography is the ability to express my own feelings in a highly individualized way with relation to a given subject. I have come to find that the process of experiencing and capturing the vision of an architect or designer through the use of light, form, and color, is in and of itself a truly rewarding experience. My work must be an enlightening, and nourishing act, and I believe that I have found that in the art of architectural photography."

**St. Judes
Research Center**
Memphis, TN
Architect
HDR

DIRECTORY

PETER AARON
ESTO PHOTOGRAPHICS
222 Valley Place
Mamaroneck, NY 10543
914.698.4060
Fax: 914.698.1033

TOM BERNARD
TOM BERNARD PHOTOGRAPHY
586 Conestoga Road
Berwyn, PA 19312
215.296.9289

GARY CIALDELLA
ARCADIA PHOTOGRAPHICS, INC.
1249 Portage Street
Kalamazoo, MI 49001
616.385.0037
Fax: 616.385.5993

CARLOS DOMENECH
CARLOS DOMENECH PHOTOGRAPHY
Miami, Florida
305.666.6964
Fax: 305.666.6964

RON FORTH
RON FORTH PHOTOGRAPHY
1507 Dana Avenue
Cincinnati, OH 45207
513.841.0858
Fax: 513.841.0858

DAVID FRANZEN
FRANZEN PHOTOGRAPHY
145 Hekili Street, Suite 100
Kailua, HI 96734
808.261.9998
Fax: 808.262.4456

JONATHAN HILLYER
JONATHAN HILLYER
PHOTOGRAPHY, INC.
2604 Parkside Drive, N.E.
Atlanta, GA 30305
404.841.6679
Fax: 404.841.9088

ANICE HOACHLANDER
HOACHLANDER PHOTOGRAPHY
ASSOCIATES
903 Girard Street NE
Washington, DC 20017
202.832.4870
Fax: 202.832.0298

TIMOTHY HURSLEY
1911 West Markham
Little Rock, AR 72205
501.372.0640
Fax: 501.372.3366

JEFFREY JACOBS
MIMSTUDIOS
2258 Young Avenue
Memphis, TN 38104
901.725.4040
Fax: 901.725.7643

THOMAS K. LEIGHTON
321 East 43rd Street
Penthouse #12
New York, NY 10017
212.370.1835

MAXWELL MacKENZIE
2641 Garfield Street, NW
Washington, DC 20008
202.232.6686
Fax: 202.232.6684

NORMAN McGRATH
NORMAN MCGRATH, PHOTOGRAPHER
164 West 79th Street
New York, NY 10024
212.799.6422
Fax: 212.799.1285

HARRISON NORTHCUTT
HARRISON NORTHCUTT
ARCHITECTURAL PHOTOGRAPHY
400 F Woodchase Lane
Marietta, GA 30067
404.980.0072
Fax: 404.980.0947

ERIC OXENDORF
ERIC OXENDORF
PHOTOGRAPHY STUDIO
1442 N. Franklin Place
P.O. Box 92337
Milwaukee, WI 53202
414.273.0654

JOCK POTTLE
ESTO PHOTOGRAPHICS
222 Valley Place
Mamaroneck, NY 10543
914.698.4060
Fax: 914.698.1033

PETER RENERTS
PETER RENERTS STUDIO
2210 Superior Viaduct
Cleveland, OH 44113
216.781.2440

CERVIN ROBINSON
251 West 92nd Street, #10E
New York, NY 10025
212.873.0464

STEVE ROSENTHAL
59 Maple Street
Auburndale, MA 02166
617.244.2986
Fax: 617.244.9824

SCOTT SANDERS
SCOTT SANDERS, PHOTOGRAPHER
9638 Sutton Green Court
Vienna, VA 22181
703.281.2538
Fax: 703.281.1071

DeANN SHIELDS-MARLEY
SHIELDS-MARLEY PHOTOGRAPHY
117 South Victory Street
Little Rock, AR 72201
501.372.6148
Fax: 501.371.9517

NICK SPRINGETT
NICK SPRINGETT PHOTOGRAPHY
1316 Maple Street
Santa Monica, CA 90405
310.271.7514

BOB SWANSON
SWANSON IMAGES
259 Clara Street
San Francisco, CA 94107
415.495.6507
Fax: 415.495.6531

BRIAN VANDEN BRINK
P.O. Box 419
Rockport, ME 04856
207.236.4035

PETER VANDERWARKER
PETER VANDERWARKER,
PHOTOGRAPHER
28 Prince Street
West Newton, MA 02165
617.964.2728

MATT WARGO
4236 Main Street
Philadelphia, PA 19127
215.483.1211
Fax: 215.483.9350

DAVID WHITTAKER
DAVID WHITTAKER
PHOTOGRAPHER, INC.
276 Carlaw Avenue, Suite #307
Toronto, Ont., Canada M4M-3L1
416.466.0558
Fax: 416.466.0989

KENNETH M. WYNER
KENNETH M. WYNER PHOTOGRAPHY
7012 Westmoreland Avenue
Takoma Park, MD 20912
301.495.9475

OTHER BOOKS

*ALSO AVAILABLE FROM RESOURCE WORLD PUBLICATIONS
AND ROCKPORT PUBLISHERS:*

Chicago Graphic Design

This new full-color volume pays overdue homage to the top design talent working in the windy city today. Teeming with talent, this midwestern metropolis graces us with some of the most formidable creativity today, including the work of Thirst, Concrete Design, Liska Associates, and Lipson Associates. The carefully selected firms have been chosen based upon their distinctive contributions to consumer, corporate, and publication design. The work showcased here transcends "regional" boundaries and explores new frontiers in design.

224 Pages, over 500 full-color images
$49.95

Hardcover with dustjacket
ISBN 1-56496-071-4

The Art of Architectural Illustration

Never before has this group of highly talented individuals been assembled in one forum to fully express their work. The book features an international cross section of "the best of the best" among architectural illustrators using a wide range of paint media. Participants from Japan, Germany, Austria, Scotland, England, Australia, Mexico, Canada, and the United States are represented. Contributors include Syd Mead, Lee Dunnette, Richard Rochon, Tom Schaller, Steve Oles, Hideo Shirai, as well as many other respected masters in the field.

226 Pages, over 400 full-color illustrations
$49.95

Hardcover with dustjacket
ISBN 1-56496-074-9

Great Landscape Architecture

The challenge of integrating man-made structure and the natural environment is one of the hallmarks of landscape architecture. *Great Landscape Architecture* features the work of leading landscape architects and firms from across the United States and Canada. Through the use of eight-page and sixteen-page portfolios, the reader is free to explore award-winning designs and projects. Included in these pages are exciting color photographs and project plans. Essays from leading authorities in the field are also presented.

300 Pages, 750 full-color images
$39.95

Hardcover with dustjacket
ISBN 1-56496-101-X

RESOURCE WORLD PUBLICATIONS, INC.
209 CENTRAL STREET, SUITE 204, NATICK, MASSACHUSETTS 01760
508.651.7000, FAX: 508.651.9950

ROCKPORT PUBLISHERS, INC.
146 GRANITE STREET, ROCKPORT, MASSACHUSETTS 01966
508.546.9590, FAX: 508.546.7141